Everyone needs beauty as well as bread, places to play in and pray in where nature may heal and cheer and give strength to body and soul alike.
—John Muir

YOSEMITE

A NATIONAL TREASURE

Produced for Yosemite Park & Curry Co.
by Albion Publishing Group, Santa Barbara, California

ALBION
PUBLISHING GROUP

Edited by Nicky Leach
Reprint Coordination by Marie Hathaway
Design by Don French and Associates
& Joanne Station
Type by Tom Buhl Typographers & LindaGraphics
Printed by Everbest Printing Company, Ltd. through
AsiaPrint/Everbest U.S.A.
ISBN: 1-880352-12-5
Library of Congress No. 88-060936

ILLUSTRATION CREDITS

Acknowledgements

Documentation for books such as this one requires a great deal of research in libraries, other books, periodicals, manuscripts, and interviews, but people are equally important. First and foremost, my thanks go to marvelous Mary Vocelka at Yosemite National Park Research Library, who was unfailingly resourceful and helpful. Her colleagues in the Yosemite Museum, Barbara Beroza and David Forgang, also provided vital photographic assistance. Other YNP staff members who read and criticized pertinent parts of the manuscript were Len McKenzie, Chief Park Interpreter; Jim Snyder, a leading YNP historian; and Craig Bates, Julia Parker, Les James, and Jay Johnson, all authorities on Yosemite's Indian History. N. King Huber, USGS geologist, lent me an advance copy of his then-unpublished *The Geologic Story of Yosemite National Park,* which was of enormous aid to my understanding and, I trust, interpretation of glacial action.

I would like to thank the Yosemite Park and Curry Co. for the opportunity to write this book. Several executives were of frequent assistance throughout this project, notably Ed Hardy, President; John Graham, Vice President, Retail; John Poimiroo, Director of Marketing; and Garrett DeBell, Environmental Consultant.

I wore out two long suffering typists, Dayle Law and Nicky Leach. The latter, my editor, retyped, red-penciled, made valid suggestions, and supplied support to me throughout the writing of this text. In addition, eagle-eye Hank Johnston, another Yosemite historian, who read and criticized the entire manuscript, not once but twice, deserves my gratitude. My last acknowledgement goes to Ginny and Jim Snyder, and Claire and Gene Kopp, who persuaded me to tackle this project, which evolved into one I enjoyed.

Shirley Sargent
Flying Spur, June 1988

Sawtooth Ridge, near Matterhorn Peak, Yosemite National Park.

CONTENTS

Clearing Winter Storm, Yosemite National Park,
California, 1944. *Photograph by Ansel Adams.*

Yosemite: The Early Years

Above: John Muir made many sketches of Yosemite formations. This one shows the view looking down Nevada canyon. Right: John Muir, circa 1910.

Within its 1,200 square miles, Yosemite National Park preserves multiple marvels—extensive, grassy meadows, towering cliffs, enormous, ancient sequoia trees, tumultuous rivers, cascading waterfalls, living glaciers, and incredible chasms. Many of these wonders are focal points in the mile-wide, seven-mile-long Yosemite Valley. For centuries, its level, river-threaded floor and combination of meadows and forests, peace and beauty was a tranquil home to wildlife and native Americans. Since 1849, when first glimpsed by non-Indians, the Valley has been an inspiration and magnet to millions of visitors who have tried to capture its glory in words, on canvas and film.

Inspiration

Inspiration Point was famous as a place where all tourists arriving from the south could get their first view of the Valley. "Here, all who make California books, down to the last and most sentimental specimen who so much as meditates a letter to his or her local paper, dismount and inflate." That was the jaundiced observation of Clarence King, a noted geologist, who claimed that he wasn't a "literary traveler," yet before long expended both rhetoric and eloquence in a book of his own. Despite such skepticism, over the years a number of people have "inflated" with words that are still memorable and quotable.

John Muir, Scotland's great gift to America, arrived in 1868 and, among other eloquent comments, penned, "No description of heaven seems half so fine," when referring to Yosemite. "This valley is the only spot that comes up to the brag and exceeds it," was essayist Ralph Waldo Emerson's 1870 comment. Two years later, outlandish showman Phineas T. Barnum made one of his usual quotable remarks while standing among the sequoias, declaring, "I told my guide I could not stand to look at a bigger tree without taking chloroform." His flippancy was soon stilled by the awesome immensities of Yosemite Valley, and his comment in a hotel register showed unexpected sensivity: Yosemite was, he said, "Unsurpassed and unsurpassable—look around with pleasure and upward with gratitude." Newspaper reporter Derrick Dodd's reaction was, "Real estate is very high hereabouts!" That bit of irreverence was countered by Emily Snow, a pioneer hotelkeeper, who boasted that the inn's site near the base of Nevada Fall was "about as near to heaven as you'll ever get."

The First Settlers

Long before such comments were made, Indians used Yosemite Valley as a seasonal sanctuary. Experts estimate that native Americans were living in the Valley as long ago as 3,000-4,000 years. The Ah-wah-ni-chi, a small tribe of Miwoks, who settled there about 800 years ago, lived harmoniously with the environment. In a sense, Indians were the first conservationists, for they protected the unusual environment with only limited usage. Their basic diet was acorns, fish, venison,

Above: Indian woman in Yosemite using a traditional baby carrier.

various greens, and fruits, their baskets made of native plants, their meager clothing largely fashioned from deer hides, and their homes, *u-ma-chas*, covered with bark from fallen cedar trees. Few traces of their long tenure in the Valley remain.

They had names for their land, *Pohono*, probably meaning "blast of wind," and *Tisaack*, a reference to an ancient Indian legend, were among the most euphonious. To them, the Valley appeared to be shaped like a mouth, for which their word was *Ahwahni*, and they were the Ahwahnichis.

Gold!

Indirectly, it was gold that resulted in the October 1849 discovery of the Valley, which was to become as precious as gold for its scenic splendor. At that time, two bear-hunting miners glimpsed the Valley peaks from a high point on the western canyon. One of them, William Penn Abrams, noted the view in his diary. The Valley, he wrote, was "enclosed by stupendous cliffs rising perhaps 3,000 feet from their base which gave us cause for wonder." Half Dome appeared to them like a loaf of bread that had been sliced by a knife. They called it Rock of Ages.

Inevitably, miners were the ones to damage the country surrounding the Valley by damming creeks and rivers, engaging in the wholesale killing of deer and other wildlife, and cutting down trees. Such practices, added to wanton shooting of Indian people and rape of their women, disrupted the lifestyle of the Miwoks. Some retaliated with raids on the miners.

A prominent trader named James D. Savage, who had befriended but manipulated the local Indians to the extent of actually marrying five or more of their women, was a victim of such a raid. After one of his stores was attacked and its staff killed, Savage helped organize the Mariposa Battalion, a band of 200 volunteers authorized by the governor of California and commanded, not surprisingly, by Savage. In March 1851, they marched into the mountains to round up all the Indians and take them to the Fresno River reservation. There was almost no resistance, but most fled for the hills of home before reaching the reser-

vation. Chief Tenaya, their leader, was an old but shrewd man whose passivity belied a passionate and proud nature.

Although the Battalion failed in its purpose, one of its companies succeeded in entering, exploring, and naming the great valley. Under the mistaken assumption that the Indians called it "Yo-sem-i-ty," Lafayette H. Bunnell, the company's young medic, named it Yo-sem-i-ty Valley. Thereafter, the men engaged in a rash of excursions into the area and bestowed what they considered fitting place-names. For example, *To-ko-ya*, became North Dome because it faced South Dome, which was soon renamed Half Dome; *To-tock-ah-noo-lah*, meaning "worm rock," was changed to El Capitan, and so forth. Chief Tenaya was far from overjoyed when Bunnell decided that Ten-ie-ya Lake should replace the Indian title, *Py-we-ack*, or "shining rock," for the high-country lake. It was obvious, Bunnell recorded, that "the naming of the lake [was] no equivalent for the loss of his territory." The chief's bitterness towards white men turned to hatred after the death of his son at their hands. The next year, Tenaya himself was killed by a rival tribe after a dispute over a gambling game.

Almost on the heels of the departing Indian people came a handful of tourists, trekking in on foot over dim trails. Eager to see if the reported cliffs and waterfalls were as sky-reaching as rumored, more people soon followed. In 1855, four parties consisting of 42 men, most of them miners, invaded. An English journalist by the name of James Mason Hutchings led the first group, which also included artist Thomas Ayres. The latter's literal paintings and Hutchings' romantic printed and reprinted descriptions put Yosemite in the minds of the traveling public. Hutchings was associated with the place, its settlement, development, and politics, until his death 48 years later.

Galen Clark, a member of the second 1855 party who had tried unsuccessfully to heal his consumptive lungs in New England, Missouri, and Texas, was so rejuvenated by the purifying air of the mountains that he lived until 1910. Both he and Hutch-

Top: Miwok acorn granaries in Yosemite Valley. Bottom: Indian men, circa 1875, stereographic detail.

Businessman Israel W. Raymond (top), Jessie Benton Fremont, wife of John C. Fremont (middle), and minister Thomas Starr King (bottom), all fought for conservation of the Mariposa Grove and Yosemite Valley.

ings were eventually buried in the Valley's Pioneer Cemetery. A year after overnighting at Wawona Meadow, a lush and logical midway stop between Mariposa and Yosemite Valley, Clark returned, resolving "to take my chances of dying or growing better which I thought were about even." Fortunately for Yosemite, he grew better. A lung hemorrhage had forced him to quit mining, but soon he began a new career, for the strategic site of his log cabin, barely off a new horse trail, plus his kindly, generous nature, propelled him (albeit reluctantly) into becoming an innkeeper. His home, which grew, he said, "as travel increased," was ramshackle, his charges inconsistent (as was his bookkeeping), but travelers appreciated shelter, bed, meals, and their quietspoken, bearded host. Besides innkeeping, he located and explored two groves of giant sequoias, which he named and publicized as the Mariposa Grove. He also befriended the local Indian people and influenced visiting VIPs with the power to effect change.

As he guided these important people to, and through, the Mariposa Grove and told them of the further wonders in Yosemite Valley, he stressed the need for their protection. Both places were undeniably unique. He wanted them safeguarded, not logged or settled by ordinary means. Already cattle and crops were detracting from the Valley's beauty.

Other men, notably minister Thomas Starr King, geologist Josiah D. Whitney, and landscape artist Frederick Law Olmsted, who was managing the vast Fremont Grant, were equally farsighted and a lot more powerful. Jessie Benton Fremont, wife of noted soldier-explorer John Fremont, who never forgot her first impression of the sequoias as "overwhelmingly grand," and Israel W. Raymond, a respected San Francisco businessman, were among the most active workers. The former bent ears while the latter attracted eyes, especially those of U.S. Senator John Conness, by giving him a set of Carleton E. Watkins' splendid photographs of the area. The culmination of all the pioneer lobbying was the congressional enactment of the Yosemite Grant. This historic act, signed by President Lincoln on June 30, 1864, gave the State of California both the irreplaceable Mariposa Grove and the incomparable Yosemite Valley to have, hold, and guard for "public use, resort, and recreation…for all time."

In effect, although managed by the State, Yosemite was a national park. Eight years later, Yellowstone was created as America's first designated national park, but the precedent, the pioneer preservationist example, was the Yosemite Grant of 1864. It was indeed a historic milestone. Homesteading, trespassing, tree-cutting, indiscriminate fires, and other injuries to natural features were unlawful.

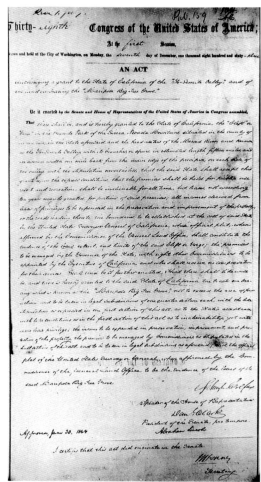

The Yosemite Grant was signed into effect by President Lincoln on June 30, 1864.

Carleton E. Watkins' photographs help convince Congress to enact the Yosemite Grant.

Wawona Tunnel in Winter.
Photograph by Ansel Adams.

Before the Grant could be officially accepted by California's governor, an eight-man Board of Commissioners, including Whitney, Raymond, Olmsted, and Clark, was named and the 39,200 acres surveyed. By fortunate chance, Olmsted, who created New York's Central Park, was in Mariposa County managing Fremont's former mines, and thus able to spend the summers of 1864-1865 in the Grant. He had the vision to formulate long-term landscape safeguards, while Clark devoted himself to day-by-day care. Both have gone down in history as selfless, dedicated men—the right ones in the right place. After the California State Legislature accepted the unprecedented gift from the nation, Galen Clark was appointed Guardian. His unselfishness in the interests of public good over private gain was admirable. Although he was a failure as a husband, father, and businessman, Clark had more than a touch of the hero about him throughout his long life.

In the depths of Yosemite Valley, 25 miles from Wawona, James Hutchings held forth as an innkeeper, tubthumper, and writer. A year after his 1855 excursion into the Valley with Thomas Ayres and others, he had begun publishing his *Hutchings' California Magazine,* a unique monthly publication portraying the varied scenes of what he termed "wonder and curiosity" in the new state. Foremost among them was Yosemite, on which he deservedly expended adjective after adjective. Although highly regarded, the magazine was hardly an economic winner. In April 1864, financially and—he claimed—physically impaired, Hutchings reclimbed the mountains, this time on defined horse trails. Earlier, he had acquired a young, unworldly wife, 22 years his junior, who was pregnant when they arrived in the Valley, and a mother-in-law, 10 years his senior. Luckily for him and the hotel guests, the latter was a capable housekeeper and cook who managed the care and feeding of guests while Hutchings served as host and nature guide. Diners were tolerant when, instead of the requested sugar bowl, he handed them, perhaps, a plate of muffins

accompanied by a rhapsodic description of a must-see wonder.

There was a bit of the humbug in Hutchings. Before the bill creating the Yosemite Grant excluding homesteading passed, but well after its intent was known, he claimed 160 acres of prime Valley land. Unlike Clark, Hutchings believed that private enterprise, especially his own, should have priority over public anything. Enraged at the Commissioners' eventual order that he must leave or pay for a lease, he did neither and for years fought them and the law by suits, lobbying, and pleas to the State Legislature and the U.S. Congress. Ultimately, he was awarded $24,000 for his holdings by the legislators, but fought eviction until 1874. He did not, however, forsake the Valley, which he genuinely loved, and continued to boost tourism with lectures illustrated by lantern slides, and books. Later, inexplicably, he was selected as Clark's successor, but served as Guardian for only one turbulent four-year term.

Other pioneers were satisfied to pay small concession fees for the privilege of operating businesses in, and above, the Valley. These enterprising folk were representative of the American "melting pot." Irishman Jim McCauley and his German Wife ran an inn atop Glacier Point, from which lofty prominence he launched a cascade of fiery embers at night. McCauley thereby established the famed Firefall, which endured on an irregular basis until 1968.

On a rocky flat near the base of Nevada Fall, New Englanders Emily and Albert Snow served their La Casa Nevada guests baked beans, doughnuts, chops, pies, and liquid refreshments. Food and spirits received enthusiastic guest comment in the inn's massive register: "No person here obliged to commit a burglary to obtain drinks..." and "Where shall I see their like again?" (in appreciation of Mrs. Snow's baked beans).

Mrs. Snow also enlivened the scene with her wry remarks. When a guest queried how they raised foods such as tomatoes, her rejoinder was a tart "on the backs of mules, ma'am, on the backs of mules."

Opposite Page, Top: Stages on Wawona Road operated between 1875 and 1915. Bottom Left: 19th-century hunters in Yosemite. Bottom Middle; Galen Clark. Photograph by George Fiske. Bottom Right: Kitty Tatch and friend on Overhanging Rock, Glacier Point. Photograph by George Fiske, circa 1890s. This Page: Famed landscape artist Frederick Law Olmsted (top) was instrumental in the creation of America's first parks. James Hutchings (above) outside his cabin in Yosemite Valley.

La Casa Nevada near Nevada Fall (top left) was run by Emily Snow (above). Other pioneer innkeepers were the McCauleys, who ran a small inn at Glacier Point (top right), James Hutchings, whose Cedar Cottage (middle) became Sentinel Hotel, and the Leidig family (bottom), who ran a popular two-story hotel in the Valley.

Inevitably, the innkeeping couple's physical presence gave validity to guides' boasts to tourists that no matter how hot and dry the summer was they would see 11 feet of Snow at their destination. Sure enough, they did, for added together, the Snows' height totaled 11 feet!

Scotswoman Isabella Leidig and her German husband Fred kept guests well-fed at their two-story hotel on the Valley floor. One breakfast menu including cat-fish and ice cream delighted John Muir. The Leidigs' 10 children appeared scare-crowish and "sadly neglected" to one woman, but they loved their parents, their home, and its freedom.

Eventually, Englishman Hutchings' former hotel evolved into a long-lived, five-unit hostelry called the Sentinel Hotel. Some plumbing was added near the turn of the century, and the Sentinel complex was not replaced until after The Ahwahnee Hotel was opened in 1927. In fact, it was 1940 before the last two buildings, one of them originally Hutchings', were torn down. Even now, the cedar tree, so long a dominant feature of his kitchen, survives.

During the pioneering years, roughly 1856-1900, comforts and conveniences were minimal in Yosemite. Rooms that resembled stalls with unbleached cotton "walls," a rude bed, a ruder mattress, a tin basin for washing, a "thundermug" (chamber pot) or a long walk to the privy, one curtainless window, and a keyless door were common, but so were good meals. After a day in a jolting stage or on a jolting horse, tourists needed no sleeping pills. Waterfalls and breezes supplied lullabies. The surroundings were so grand, the view so superb, that complaints were rare. For years, the tourist season was largely between April and July while water was high and dust and heat low. Between 1855 and 1868, total recorded visitation was fewer than 3,000 persons. More than 1,100 came in 1869, the year the transcontinental railroad opened, but it was 1899 before "crowds" topped 4,000. Until stage roads replaced trails in 1874 and 1875, saddle animals remained the mode of transportation around the Valley. It was Mirror Lake one

day, Bridalveil Fall the next, not forgetting a trek to Vernal Fall and Nevada Fall another day, plus aches and pains in between.

After 1874, such complaints could be relieved by a blissful immersion in honest-to-goodness bathtubs! One female author was astonished to find "Sybaritic arrangements," and "baths of balm, delicious soothing and healing...." All this and much, much more was available in John Smith's Cosmopolitan Saloon and Bathhouse. "The attraction of the baths," wrote British artist Constance F. Gordon-Cumming, "are greatly enhanced by the excellence of the iced drinks...a running accompaniment of brandy cocktails, gin slings, 'barber's poles...,' 'Samson with the hair on,' 'corpse revivers,' 'rattlesnakes,' and other potent, picturesquely named combinations."

Bar and billiard rooms were the domain of men, but the thoughtful Mr. Smith had reserved one of the five bathrooms and a small, perfectly appointed sitting room for the ladies. Like the Snows' provisions, all of the Cosmopolitan's furnishings had arrived on the backs of mules. Beasts of burden, indeed!

Other business establishments in the same village complex as the Cosmopolitan were designed to relieve visitors of coin rather than fatigue and grime. Items from sequoia seeds to horseshoes, pillows stuffed with pine needles to pincushions, photographs to telegrams were available in the dozen or so shops along Main Street, the one and only street of the Upper Village. (Lower Village, near the base of the Four-Mile-Trail, was far smaller and after 1915, nonexistent.)

Variety predominated at the Upper Village's general store. A three-and-a-half pound can of coffee cost $1.00, as did three cans of apricots or six pounds of soda crackers. A pound of ham was 23 cents, 10 pounds of salt 50 cents, and a gallon of Golden Drip Syrup $1.25. Fresh meat from the butcher shop ranged in cost from beef, 20 to 25 cents per pound, to mutton, 12 to 15 cents. Across the road at Degnan's Bakery, run by an Irish couple, a loaf of bread was priced at 25 cents; pies the same.

John Smith (top) provided "baths of balm, delicious, soothing and healing . . .," as well as iced drinks for weary, dusty travelers at his Cosmopolitan Saloon and Bathhouse (above).

Above Left: Bridgeport Tom and family, circa 1902. Photograph by J. T. Boysen. Above Right: From left to right, Susan and John Lawrence (brother and sister), Sally Ann Dick and Johnny Dick (brother and sister). Photograph by George Fiske.

By the 1870s, local Indian people numbered fewer than 50, with many of them working in, or for, the hotels: the women as maids, kitchen or laundry help, the men as woodcutters, fishermen, stablemen, or laborers on trails and roads. Their assimilation into the non-Indian community was limited. Their villages of rough board-bark-and-canvas structures stood apart, away from the new settlers. Even their costume of layers of cast-off clothing exhibited lack of social and economic integration. Their culture had been completely disrupted through contact with settlers and tourists but many traditions survived. Acorns remained basic to their diet, and most of the women still wove beautiful baskets. Not only were they utilitarian, but by the 1890s, so salesworthy that the women began making them to sell to tourists as well.

Visitor needs and desires had altered not only the Indians' harmonious way of life, but the very environment that made Yosemite Valley a world wonder. Protection and preservation were the keynote of the Yosemite Grant, yet intent was not being fully realized by the State Administration. Visitors expected meals composed of milk, meat, and eggs, so the population of farmyard animals such as cattle, hogs, and chickens proliferated. Fences crisscrossed the meadows containing crops of hay and grain, which had replaced native grasses. Barbed wire separated herds of horses, pack animals, and burros. Few people used their legs for anything more ambitious than maintaining balance in saddles during the obligatory sightseeing trips.

Muir of the Mountains

John Muir was one of the rare, but increasing, breed of people who walked, tramped, and explored nature's loveliness. In 1868, as an aimless, 30-year-old Scottish wanderer, he had walked from Oakland, California, to Yosemite, where lifelong love and work awaited him. During the following year, he tramped behind 2,000 sheep as they ate their destructive way up from the foothills to the 8,600-foot high Tuolumne Meadows. "The harm they do goes to the heart," he recounted in his journal. "To let sheep trample so divinely fine a place seems barbarous...." Stopping that destruction became a purpose. Studying what he was convinced was the "...united labors of the grand combination

of glaciers..." in creating the meadows, canyons, and domes of Yosemite was soon established as another goal. His aimlessness evaporated as his lifework became clear. He needed time for study and observations, but daily bread was also a necessity. Therefore, that fall, he "sold" himself, as he put it, to innkeeper Hutchings "...to feed sows and turkeys, build hen roosts, laying boxes, etc." Hutchings needed a sawmill to produce lumber for improvements and additions to his hotel. Muir, whose inventiveness had won him praise and prizes in Wisconsin, assembled and operated the water-powered mill.

Logging, at least in the Valley, was not a by-product of development. Periodic violent winds, known as Mono winds, had devastated the forests, uprooting and felling both weak and healthy trees. These extensive blowdowns supplied Muir with a huge stockpile of logs. No live trees were cut by the budding conservationist, and the job enabled him to remain in the Valley, absorbing nature even as he hauled and cut timber. When he wasn't working, he was earning a reputation for eccentricity and fearlessness. His passion for his surroundings was such that he began guiding VIPs,

writing articles, and eventually making speeches, all with the ever-growing intent,

> *...to show forth the beauty, grandeur, and all-embracing usefulness of our wild mountain forests, reservations and parks, with a view to inciting people to come and enjoy them, and get them into their hearts that so at length their preservation and right use might be made sure.*

After 1874, Muir was lured away to explore the entire Sierra Nevada and Alaska, to write, and to marry and raise a family. No matter where he was or what he did, Yosemite remained his passion, and his frequent return visits not only refreshed but dismayed him.

Top Left: John Muir's sketch of the southwest side of Cathedral Spur in the backcountry near Mt. Lyell. Top Right: John Muir in August 1895 near Hetch Hetchy. Photograph by T.P. Lukens. Middle: This sawmill was operated by John Muir for James Hutchings. Above: James Hutchings in old age.

The Creation of Yosemite National Park

Right: A rare 1870s view of Crane Flat on the way to Yosemite. Gobins Hotel (left of Big Oak Flat Road) and Billy Hurst's Saloon (upper right) provided basic beds and refreshments for travelers.

No one, not even the participants, could have foretold the dramatic consequences of a sightseeing trip in June 1889. At that time, a prestigious New York magazine editor named Robert Underwood Johnson arrived in the Valley accompanied by his friend and uniquely qualified guide, John Muir, who had not been there since 1884. Even then he had been scornful at the abundance of crops and buildings. Instead of browsing deer, cattle grazed. Instead of coyotes' howls, the barking of dogs and crowing of roosters resounded.

Money-grubbers and politicians were in the temple! Many outraged Californians knew it and were making waves. Earlier in 1889, a State committee had held inconclusive hearings in the Valley on 22 charges of mismanagement by the Yosemite Commissioners. Each time a new governor was elected, new board members and usually a new guardian, most of them "fat cats" who had aided the governor, were appointed. Appropriations for improvements on such essential items as trails, roads, and bridges were niggardly to nonexistent. Clear-cut, honest administration seemed impossible.

Early in June, the month of the Muir and Johnson visit, the incumbent guardian was summarily sacked. After lengthy deliberation, a new one, considered to be the soul of integrity and a great lover of nature who would not allow "natural beauties to be ruthlessly destroyed [for] pecuniary profit," was selected. The new guardian was sober, selfless, 75-year-old Galen Clark! Muir probably applauded the appointment, but knew, as did Clark, that the Legislature still held the purse strings, and preservation had never been a priority with them.

"The Valley," Muir thundered," looked like a frowsy, backwoods pasture." The pretentious, three-story hotel that had replaced pioneer inns, had, he said, "a silly look amid surroundings so massive and sublime."

They climbed the mountains to Tuolumne Meadows and found that nature's peace had been diminished by sheep and cattle even there.

Muir was heartsick. In 1869, he had written of the "hoofed locusts," and the harm they did to grasses and flowers. He had been unknown and powerless to do anything then to halt the seasonal invasion of the four-legged meadow mowers. Now, with his reputation as a preservationist, people would be sure to read and listen to his persuasive words. Johnson, editor of *Century* magazine and a man who had access to influential citizens, including politicians, all over the East Coast, would be his strongest ally. That night, warmed by a campfire and their indignation, the two men planned a campaign to make the high country surrounding Yosemite Valley into a national park. Amazingly, their labors, which were considerable, were rewarded barely 13 months later when, on October 1, 1890, the U.S. Congress created Yosemite National Park.

John Muir and editor Robert Underwood Johnson were appalled by animals grazing in Yosemite Valley (top) and land claimants plowing up the Valley floor near Kenneyville, site of the present Ahwahnee Hotel (above).

The Cavalry Takes Charge

As in Yellowstone National Park, U.S. Army units were appointed as seasonal caretakers of the new Park. Cavalrymen waged war against sheepmen and their thousands of fleecy, chomping charges in the high country. It took several summers before a successful campaign to separate herders from flocks evolved. After arresting herders, troopers escorted them to a remote area and then freed them on foot into the wilds. At the same time, other troopers drove the "meadow mowers" from the Park to an equally distant place. Even then, many herders and their flocks eluded capture because they knew the hidden recesses of the high country. Eventually, maps and trails were developed by the cavalrymen, and the sheepmen were forced to use other pastures outside the Park boundaries.

Camp A.E. Wood, army headquarters, was on a flat a mile or so north of Wawona, but small groups of cavalrymen were stationed at patrol camps at many sites in the new Park. They surveyed and marked the boundaries, blazed and built trails and bridges, stocked lakes and rivers with fish, made maps, fought fires, confiscated guns, and often spent 16 to 20 hours a day tending to their work. Their accomplishments under the guidance of top-notch officers were of tremendous benefit to Yosemite National Park.

Conflict with the lackadaisical state administration of the Yosemite Grant, a small park within a large park, was inevitable. For example, fires crossed boundaries that men weren't allowed to; and soldiers had the power to disarm hunters, but Valley residents could use firearms. Gradually it dawned on even proud Californians that only federal administration could assure a unified and truly protected national park. Inevitably, too, Muir led the battle for California to re-cede the land given it by the federal government in 1864. He alerted editor Johnson, who would again be his powerfully ally, as to the Valley's plight.

It looks ten times worse now than when you saw it seven years ago. Most of the level meadow floor of the Valley is fenced with barbed and unbarbed wire and about three hundred head of horses are turned loose every night to feed and trample the flora out of existence. I told the hotel and horsemen that they were doing all they could to prevent lovers of wild beauties from visiting the Valley....

Johnson was not Muir's only renowned supporter. The united lobbying of the Sierra Club, which Muir had helped to found in 1892, was a force for recession, and of course, he could count on President Theodore Roosevelt, who had been mightily impressed with the naturalist on their 1903 camping tour of the Grant. In the bitter end, however, it was Muir's unlikely friend, railroad magnate Edward H. Harriman, whose pointed political letters and telegrams eased the passage of the recession bill through by only one vote in the California Senate. Then, in 1906, it was again Harriman who persuaded—or maybe intimidated—the House of Representatives and Senate to vote "yes" on the acceptance bill, which President Roosevelt signed into existence on June 11, 1906. After that, Yosemite Valley and the Mariposa Grove were the crown jewels of Yosemite National Park.

1906—A Momentous Year

That year, 1906, was notable for two other literally earthshaking events that affected Yosemite. On April 18, a disastrous earthquake and resultant fire devastated San Francisco and the Bay Area. Visitation to Yosemite decreased from 10,000 in 1905 to 5,414 in 1906, as Northern Californians struggled to put their lives back together. Moreover, banks, hotels, and transportation lines were disrupted for months after the cataclysm, daunting even travelers from the East.

Nevertheless, construction of the Yosemite Valley Railroad from Merced to El Portal, 12 miles west of Yosemite Valley, progressed. That "Shortline to Paradise," which made its first run on May 15, 1907, provided the first convenient access to Yosemite Valley and opened the way for the flood of sightseers that continues to this day. Not only would queens, kings, and

Above: Camp A.E. Wood, near Wawona, was army headquarters for the cavalrymen who patrolled the new Yosemite National Park until the creation of the National Park Service. Left: The Glacier Point Hotel was one of the hotels that replaced the original pioneering inns in Yosemite.

Above: President Theodore Roosevelt visited Yosemite in May 1903. John Muir (seen here with Roosevelt on Glacier Point) took him camping in the Yosemite backcountry and persuasively made the case for conservation of America's wilderness areas. Right: Half Dome looms over a Yosemite guide, high above the Valley floor on Glacier Point. Photograph by Ansel Adams.

presidents travel aboard the trains, but supplies of every kind and size needed by the Army and concessionaires were regularly shipped via rail. It was not long after the advent of the railroad that the need for freight wagons, and the army of horses and mules needed to pull them, was greatly reduced. Stages, however, continued to be used daily until 1914.

In June 1906, the third significant date of that year, Yosemite Valley officially became part of Yosemite National Park. Immediately afterwards, War Department officials telegraphed Captain Harry C. Benson, the 42-year-old commanding officer of the Sixth Cavalry at Wawona, to take charge. Nothing could have pleased the future colonel more. Under his firm control, army headquarters was moved into the Valley to the site later occupied by Yosemite Lodge. Tents, officers' quarters, stables, forage houses, grain sheds, and orderly rooms had to be built, or reassembled, by the troopers, under the direction of one harried civilian carpenter.

After Fort Yosemite was established, the soldiers' first attack was on sanitation, or rather the lack of it. Five public camp-

grounds, three of them adjacent to meadows where campers pastured their horses and mules, were closed because none boasted so much as a privy. A number of campers complained, but Benson and his troops were interested in creating good practices, not good will. Their battles with concessionaires, who allowed raw sewage to pollute the river, gained additional censure. Some residents were angered when their firearms and animal traps were taken away, but Benson wanted to teach wildlife "that the Valley is a safe retreat and not a death trap." Up until then, he reported, "Practically every person living in the Valley kept a rifle, shotgun, and revolver, and any animal or bird that was unfortunate enough to enter…was immediately pursued by the entire contingent, and captured or killed."

A New Era of Transportation

Although the first automobile entered Yosemite Valley in June 1900, it was August 1913 before cars were finally permitted on a regular basis. Even then, the mounted Cavalry posted and enforced restrictive speed limit conditions of 10 m.p.h. in "rolling, mountain country," 5 m.p.h. on steep descents, and 15 m.p.h. on the Valley floor. Guards fined drivers $1.00 per mile if they arrived earlier or later than the alloted time between check stations. Despite restrictions, 739 automobiles entered the Valley in the year 1914, and 2,270 in 1915.

Surprisingly, John Muir, master pedestrian, approved the new mode of transportation. He commented:

Doubtless, under certain precautionary restrictions these useful, progressive, blunt-nosed mechanical beetles will hereafter be allowed to puff their way into all the parks and mingle their gas breath with the breath of the pines and waterfalls, and, from the mountaineer's standpoint, with but little harm or good."

Actually, the "blunt-nosed beetles" did do good because their proliferating usage cut down on the number of horses and mules hitherto coming in on stage roads or required to carry or haul visitors from the train station. Slowly, the meadow grasses grew back, stages and buggies were retired, and a number of barns emptied. A Red Lion gas station was built and storage tanks installed underground; however, "gas breath" did not yet equate smog or smell any worse than manure at the turn of the century.

The Birth of the National Park Service

By 1914, the United States of America boasted 12 national parks and 19 national monuments, most of them patrolled and administered by the War Department. As cavalrymen were needed for more important duty, particularly action in World War I, than chasing sheep or fining automobile drivers, 1914 was their last season in Yosemite. Back in the political halls of Washington, D.C., the Department of the Interior realized that a new, year-round governmental bureau was necessary to replace the troops. Coincidentally, a Chicago business tycoon, 47-year-old Stephen T. Mather, complained of the ways the parks were being run to his friend, Interior Secretary Franklin K. Lane. In an oft-quoted reply, Lane wrote, "Dear Steve: If you don't like the way the national parks are run, why don't you come down to Washington and run them yourself?"

In December 1914, Mather went to the capital and agreed to do just that if a young Interior Department lawyer, Horace M. Albright, would aid him for a year: Albright stayed for 29 years! Mather, the visionary, and Albright, the realist, gathered together disciples and, 21 months later, steered a bill through Congress and the Senate that created the National Park Service. The text of the bill was simple and straightforward, echoing both the meaning and wording of its predecessor act in creating the original Yosemite Grant in 1864.

Opposite Page; Mass transportation, such as these "Rubbernecker" buses (top), appeared in Yosemite in the 1930s. Stages and buggies (middle) gradually gave way to automobiles, which first entered the Park in 1913. The Wawona Tunnel (bottom left) was finished in 1933. A motorcyclist (bottom right) studies the initials carved on the walls of the Wawona tunnel tree, circa 1920. Above: Stephen Mather, first director of the National Park Service, showing his friend, Interior Secretary Franklin K. Lane, around Yosemite.

Above: Horace M. Albright, co-founder of the National Park Service. Below: Eleanor Roosevelt, shown here with Yosemite National Park rangers, was a tremendous supporter of conservation and equal opportunity, both key elements of today's National Park Service. Right: Winter scene in Yosemite. Photograph by Ansel Adams.

In 1916, the primary intention of the National Park Service was, as it still is, "to conserve the scenery and the natural and historic objects and the wildlife therein and to provide for the enjoyment of the same in such a manner and by such means as will leave them unimpaired for the enjoyment of future generations."

The new bureau was responsible for the management of 16 national parks and 21 national monuments, a total now expanded to 49 parks, 77 monuments, and 212 other preserved areas of national importance. These units vary from national battlefields and rivers to seashores and the White House. Each place is administered by a superintendent who oversees a staff of rangers. Before long, duties were divided between a protective force in charge of law enforcement, and an interpretive branch in charge of interpreting natural and human history by way of lectures, nature walks, exhibits, and publications.

At first, a woman in a ranger's uniform was a rarity; today, women fill many different positions, including that of park superintendent. Yosemite had a woman ranger as early as 1918. Its first female assistant superintendent was appointed in 1987.

Today, dedicated men and women continue to fight the good, and often frustrating, fight to preserve our resources begun by Stephen T. Mather, 1867-1930, and Horace M. Albright, 1890-1987. Both parks and people benefit, and as Muir wrote, "we are rich forever."

Distant Beginnings

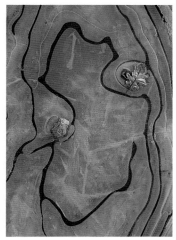

Above: Leaves and ice combine to make an abstract pattern during winter in Yosemite. Right: A spectacular view of Half Dome from Glacier Point, showing the glacial legacy of the Sierra Nevada.

It was well into the 1860s before Josiah Dwight Whitney, the Yale-trained California State Geologist, thought he had the answers to widespread questions as to the origin of Yosemite Valley. Despite evidence of glaciation, he claimed that the creation of the Valley was due to a natural catastrophe when, "the bottom of the Valley sank down to an unknown depth, owing to its support being withdrawn from underneath." A college dropout almost 20 years Whitney's junior disputed the distinguished geologist. "Whitney says that the bottom has fallen out of the rocks here," John Muir wrote, "which I most devoutly disbelieve." "Glaciers," he explained from atop Glacier Point, had "labored, and cut and carved, and elaborated, until they have wrought out this royal road." Obstinately, Whitney pronounced the upstart an "ignoramus," and "a mere shepherd."

Actually, Muir had had some training in glaciation while at the University of Wisconsin. That background and two years of intensive on-site studies helped him form his controversial theory, which had been originally introduced by the Swiss-born Louis Agassiz before he began teaching at Harvard in 1848. Muir studied Agassiz's revolutionary ideas in Wisconsin, and applied them to his own investigations of ice, rocks, and debris in Yosemite. Eventually, one of Muir's letters to Agassiz elicited his admiring comment: "Here is the first man who has an adequate conception of glacial action."

Although overestimating the extent of glaciation and underestimating the role of rivers in shaping the landscape, Muir's interpretations were far more accurate than those of Whitney. Some of the physical features that alerted Muir to the true origin of the Valley can be recognized even now from an automobile in Yosemite Valley. For example, a low ridge, composed of rubble deposited by a glacier, is particularly obvious in a road cut west of El Capitan on the north side of the Valley, and in another road cut east of Bridalveil Meadow on the south side of the Valley. Technically, the ridge is known as a terminal moraine, as it marks the end, or terminus, of an ancient glacier. Later the ridge served as a dam for a subsequent lake, and eventually impeded the flow of the Merced River.

Power

Agassiz had likened glaciers to gargantuan plows. Muir adopted this concept, not recognizing the immense erosive forces of the river prior to glaciation. N. King Huber, author of *The Geologic Story of Yosemite National Park* published in 1987, explained the importance of flowing water in shaping the environment. "About 15 million years ago, the Yosemite area had a rolling surface of rounded hills and broad valleys with meandering streams. By 10 million years ago, uplift of the range was sufficient to steepen stream gradients, and valleys deepened. Before the onset of glaciation possibly some 2 million years ago, streams had incised deep canyons

Above: The Merced River Canyon is a good example of a V-shaped canyon, eroded by a river rather than glacial ice. Right: Glacial polish is created by the smoothing action of glaciers as they pass over rock.

into the west flank of the range." The Merced River Canyon, west of Yosemite Valley, is a striking example of a deeply incised, unglaciated canyon.

Glaciers

Glaciers were a modifying agent in the deepening and widening of Yosemite Valley during many individual glaciations. Glaciers are formed when heavy winter snow combines with a persistently cold climate for a century or more. "At a thickness of about 100 feet," Huber wrote, "ice begins to flow outward under its own weight, and on slopes will begin to flow downhill at lesser thicknesses; when it flows, a glacier is born." The glacier's seasonal snowline, or technically, "firn limit," can be far below the mountain peaks. A glacier's prolonged death begins when the climate changes and turns drier or warmer. Muir commented that the life of a glacier was "one eternal grind."

A succession of glaciations shaped much of Yosemite National Park. The last major one, called the Tioga glaciation, began somewhere between 30,000 and 60,000 years ago, and peaked 15,000 to 20,000 years back. Its icy fingers spread from the range crest to the floor of Yosemite Valley. It did little to change Yosemite Valley, however, as it had been sculpted largely by earlier, more extensive glaciers.

A glacier's corrosive action, the smoothing and "plucking" evidenced by still-present imprints of glacial striations, a kind of marking on the rock, and polish, is determined by the velocity and depth of the ice.

The formation of Yosemite (counterclockwise from top left): Yosemite was originally an area of rolling hills, broad valleys, and meandering streams, until about 10 million years ago, when periodic uplifting of the range caused the stream gradients to steepen and erode the valleys into deep canyons. Possibly some two million years ago, a succession of glaciers filled the Yosemite Valley and High Sierra area, causing a widening of the deep valleys into U-shaped canyons and the creation of splendid waterfalls. Lake Yosemite was formed after the Yosemite Valley glacier melted. Today, Yosemite Valley is green and fertile, bisected by the Merced River.

Above: A legacy of extensive glaciation in the Valley, Yosemite Falls is shown here in springtime at the peak of its flow. Right: Half Dome. Opposite: El Capitan is a magnificient reminder of the awesome sculpting power of glaciers.

Jointing

The distinctive features of the Valley landmarks, the sheer face of El Capitan, the arches of Royal Arches, the rounded summit of Sentinel Dome, and the sloping surfaces on the back side of the Three Brothers, were determined by the fracturing or "jointing" of the granite and modified by the massive impact of glacial ice.

According to Huber, "Joints are an overwhelming influence on landform development...because they form greatly contrasting zones of weakness in otherwise homogeneous, erosion-resistant rock and are avenues of access of water and air for weathering.... Vertical joint sets are responsible for the orientation of major features, such as the planar face of Half Dome and the series of parallel cliffs at Cathedral Rocks."

Half Dome

Even at its deepest, approximately 3,000 feet thick, the ice never covered the tops of Clouds Rest, Half Dome, and El Capitan. Contrary to popular belief, Half Dome is now considered to be relatively unchanged from the time of its formation. About 80 percent of its impressive body is still there; the rest was hewn away by the frost-splitting of rock at the base of the cliff. The prevalent visual impression "that this is a round dome which had lost its northwest half is an illusion," Huber said.

Besides splendid sculpting, glaciers also created the "hanging" valleys along the uneven rims of Yosemite Valley. From these sloping stream channels erupt the astonishing waterfalls that are as famous as Yosemite's cliffs and domes. Most of the waterfalls are each a single fall, such as Bridalveil, but Yosemite Falls is a series of three falls, totalling 2,425 feet in height, making it "falls" rather than a "fall." Seven major waterfalls pour over the granite walls to supply a visual feast to Park visitors, and then flow west to serve as irrigation water to California's vast fruit-basket, better known as the San Joaquin Valley.

Nothing but Rocks

A woman who visited Yosemite Valley during a dry autumn, when not so much as a drop of water slipped over Yosemite Falls, was put out. "We drove clear across the country to see this place," she complained, "and there's nothing but rocks!"

She was partially right, of course. There was nothing but the most colossal, magnificently shaped cliffs and domes, nothing but the most famous rocks in the world, towering above her. "Great is granite and Yosemite is its prophet," author J. Smeaton Chase stated in 1911. Granite is prodigal in Yosemite, and most of the many kinds take their names from prominent features. Thus, there's El Capitan Granite, Taft Granite, Half Dome Grandiorite, and so on. All are igneous, formed when magma (hot, molten material beneath the Earth's surface), cooled and solidified.

U-Shaped Valleys

While glaciers were transforming Yosemite Valley from a V-shaped canyon into a seven-mile long, half-mile wide U-shaped trough, similar landscape modifications were occurring elsewhere in the area. Hetch Hetchy, long dammed yet part of Yosemite National Park, is an amazingly similar though somewhat smaller replica of Yosemite Valley. Little Yosemite Valley is another, though less obvious, example with a river-threaded grassy "floor." The lovely, lively Lyell Canyon also slowly evolved into a U-shaped valley. Even today, the Lyell Fork of the Tuolomne River is partially fed by the melt of the remnants of Mt. Lyell's and Mt. Maclure's glaciers. Lyell, the larger of the two, covers less than a quarter square mile. Mt. Dana's small glacier feeds into Tioga Lake.

Tuolumne Meadows

In 1869, when John Muir first saw the meadows and domes of this expansive and serenely beautiful high country, he exulted, "A fine region this, to study glaciers." It still is. Rounded domes, "erratic" rocks, glacial "polish," and "kettle" ponds are as abundant as they are interesting and beautiful. An erratic is a boulder that a glacier carried from a great distance and left isolated, commonly on a completely different kind of bedrock. Good examples can be observed on the granite slope above Olmsted Point, where melting ice stranded rocks of various compositions. Kettles are small lakes or ponds that fill depressions created by ice melt. Several mirror the sky near Tioga Pass. Glacial polish (glistening rock) is particularly outstanding on the granite domes near Tenaya Lake. No wonder Chief Tenaya named the area *Pyweack*, meaning "shining rocks."

Top: Lake Hetch Hetchy today. Bottom: Hetch Hetchy Valley looked like a smaller version of Yosemite Valley before it was dammed. Right: Glacial erratic boulders are fascinating reminders of Yosemite's geological past. Far Right: Tuolumne Meadows, in the Yosemite high country, is remarkable for its peaceful, river-threaded scenery, surrounding glacial domes, and wildlife.

Above: Tioga Lake, bordering Yosemite, is a popular destination of hikers in the high country above Yosemite Valley. Right: Tenaya Lake at sunset. For Right: Vernal Fall (and its neighbor, Nevada Fall), created by Yosemite's unique geological past, are within moderate hiking distance of Yosemite Village.

Glacial Lakes

Gem-like Tenaya Lake nestles at the base of a 7,000-foot bowl gouged by a branch of the Tuolumne Glacier. The Tioga Road borders it on the north, making it the most accessible lake in the Park. Windsurfers, sailboaters, swimmers, fishermen, campers, picnickers, and gulls enjoy its mile-long, half-mile-wide expanse during summer days. May Lake, at the base of Mt. Hoffmann, is another post-glacial lake. All of Yosemite's 300-400 lakes are transitory, destined to silt in and become meadows, as have many before them. Meanwhile, some are repositories for trout and are beautifully framed by a variety of rock formations. They are appreciated by fishermen and hikers alike.

What Next?

Although the present Sierra Nevada has been developing for a period in excess of 15 million years, its history is far from complete. In addition to weathering and erosion, glaciers, earthquakes, and subsequent rock slides are tremendous modifying agents. Recently, volcanic activity has occurred near Mono Lake and Mammoth Lakes, on the east side of the Park. That activity, experts warn, is likely to continue for many years to come.

At this time, the most recent ice age has ended. Ancient Lake Yosemite has been filled with sediment, allowing the growth of grasses and trees in the ever-evolving Yosemite Valley. The "living glaciers" that so excited Muir in the 1870s have shrunk. The Sierra Nevada is one of the fastest-growing mountain ranges on Earth, rising at an inch every thousand years, but modification continues in inchworm fashion. Uplift and erosion persevere, and some time in the remote, virtually unimaginable future, erosion will outpace uplift, and the Sierra will again be reduced to rolling upland. In the millenia before that happens, Yosemite's beauty and diversity will provide enchantment, particularly for those who study even rudimentary geology.

The Four Seasons of Yosemite

Spring

The Glory
of Nature

*Above: Western greathorn owl.
Right: Flowering dogwood and
pine trees.*

lthough outwardly rugged in
appearance and filled with a vast
array of fabulous wildlife,
Yosemite comprises a very fragile eco-
system that is constantly at risk from both
nature and man. Root rot is a wholesale
killer of trees, especially in Yosemite Valley.
Until recent legislation passed, low-flying
airplanes threatened safety and disturbed
wildlife and visitors. Forest fires can be
catastrophic. It is no longer safe to drink
from creeks and lakes, as *Giardia Lamblia*,
which causes a painful, intestinal disease,
is in much of the water. And bears can be a
nuisance. All those and other concerns,
partly caused by humans, interfere with
but do not halt the evolutionary domi-
nance of nature.

No matter how sophisticated, lasting,
and intricate man's technological achievements appear, nature's peace alternates
with a fury that continually alters the
environment. Earthquake-caused rock
slides killed three hikers, injured eight,
and forced closure of two popular trails in
1980. Not even the Queen of England could
enter the Valley on either the slide-blocked
All-Year Highway (140), or the Wawona
Road (41) in March 1983. Queen Elizabeth
II and Prince Philip had to be ushered in
around lesser slides on the Big Oak Flat
Road (120) for their two-day visit. Record-
breaking snowfall and heavy rains then,
and again in 1986, caused Park-wide property damage and flooding, but also
resulted in waterfalls of great volume and
beauty. "The snow," John Muir said, "is melting into music." Even as nature dominates

and devastates, it provides the prodigal
and diverse attractions that continue to
magnetize millions of awed visitors.

Giants of the Earth

It was Ralph Waldo Emerson, the sage
of New England, who in 1871 reacted to the
aged, massive, towering sequoia trees in
the Mariposa Grove by saying, "The wonder of it is that we can see these trees and
not wonder more." If one enormous
sequoia, say 250 feet high and 15 feet in
diameter, stood in the middle of a meadow,
onlookers would be on their knees in awe.
Viewed in the ranks and clusters of the
Mariposa Grove, in the company of perhaps as many as 600 other giants, astonish-
ment and awe are curiously lessened by
their very multitude. These trees that
Emerson said had "a monstrous talent for
growing tall," are one of the wonders of the
world. A tram ride or a walk among them
inspires amazement. Not only their size
but their age is impressive. The venerable
Grizzly Giant, whose lower branches are
larger in diameter than most pine trees, is
estimated to be 2,700 years old. Its cin-
namon-colored trunk was thrusting sky-
ward at the time of Christ, growing long
before Mount Vesuvius erupted in A.D. 79,
or the Crusades took place in the second
century A.D. Preservation of the Mariposa
Grove, first publicized by Galen Clark in
1857, was one of the primary reasons the
State-administered Yosemite Grant was
created in 1864. Its magnificence would be
safeguarded forever from human exploitation. Fire suppression proved to be inju-

rious, however, as it allowed the growth of other species, primarily pines, incense cedar, and white fir, to become dense, and the pileup of flammable undergrowth increased fire danger. Propagation of sequoia trees was prevented by the covering of the mineral soil. In recent years, to simulate the natural process that had played a vital role in forest ecology, the Park Service has instituted an often controversial program of prescription burning to augment and advance time-consuming and expensive clearing by axes and saws.

Years before the creation of Yosemite National Park protected them, two more groves of sequoias were discovered and explored. Exploration did not take long as there are only 29 mammoth trees in the Tuolumne Grove, and 20 in the Merced Grove. Trees in these groves were described as "incredibly large" by a diary-keeping member of the Walker party in 1833. When rival stage roads to Yosemite were being built in the early 1870s, the Big Oak Flat and Yosemite Turnpike Company routed its toll way through the Tuolumne Grove and later cut a tunnel through the Dead Giant. Of course, that grove soon became a popular stage stop because of the new attraction.

Not to be outdone, the Coulterville and Yosemite Turnpike Company built its road through the Merced Grove, which one of its surveyors had discovered. Both turnpikes opened in 1874. The latter still exists but is now bumpy and little-travelled, while the former was replaced by the modern Big Oak Flat Road (Highway 120) in 1940. Between Crane Flat and the Big Oak Flat Entrance Station, the section passing through the Tuolumne Grove has been retained as a one-way road. It is still possible for visitors to walk or drive through the Dead Giant. Beyond the grove, the route is bordered by a veritable forest of dogwood flowers, enchantingly white with bloom in April and May and red-leafed in October and November.

A Feast of Forests

Besides the sequoia groves, Yosemite constitutes a tree-lover's paradise. Its terrain varies in elevation from 2,000 feet in

the Merced River Canyon, where live oaks, buckeyes, and digger pines cling to the rocky slopes, to ponderosa pine, Douglas fir, incense cedar, scattered sugar pines around Wawona and Yosemite Valley, craggy red fir, and aspen above 6,000 feet, white and red fir and a prevalence of lodgepole pines around Tuolumne Meadows and Glacier Point, and the tenacious whitebark pine just below the treeline. Jeffrey pine and gnarled juniper are also hardy high country dwellers, the rarer knobcone is happy at lower elevations.

Ponderosa pines are the preeminent trees in Yosemite Valley. Their neatly furrowed bark, resembling pieces of a puzzle, encases a stately trunk that terminates in symmetrical branches 100 to 150 feet above the ground. Campers pitch tents or park recreation vehicles under their shade, and love to hear the wind sing in the boughs. Shelter and sound may end soon as the shallow-rooted ponderosas, infected with root rot by a fungus called *Fomes annosus*, die. Not only are they threatened, but their demise would endanger humans.

Since 1852, five destructive 40 to 80 m.p.h. winds (known as Mono winds) have felled hundreds of pines, which, in crashing down, have killed five people,

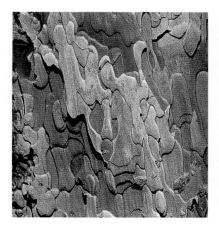

injured 11, and smashed 118 structures and 36 vehicles. Thus nature and man, by defensive logging, are rapidly removing hazardous trees. Some experts predict that most of the conifers on the Valley's floodplain will be dead by the year 2007. Already, Valley campgrounds have bare, bald, unshaded sites, but eventually oak trees will again become dominant.

Each tree, from sugar pines, which Muir called "kings of the forest," to mountain mahogany, a pygmy, have beauty, charm, and purpose. Principally, their roots retain water, forestall erosion, and act as an air conditioner. Birds flock to the forest supermarket to shop. Seeds, acorns, and insects are their staff of life. Even the ubiquitous Steller's jays, familiar as "camp robbers," love acorns as well as peanuts.

Fine-Feathered Friends

Yosemite has harbored 232 species of birds whose songs, antics, and appetites interest even the most casual visitor. Two endangered species, the great gray owl and the peregrine falcon, are migratory visitors. For centuries, falcons have awed observers with their speed, up to 200 m.p.h., aerial displays, and fierce appearance. Once populous in many areas, fewer than 40 pairs are estimated as remaining in California. Two pairs of those precious few nest in Yosemite and biologists are practicing "nest augmentation," by trading peregrine chicks hatched in captivity for the DDT-damaged eggs found in the nests. Those eggs are examined for DDT-shell-thinning, and, if viable, hatched under scientific care. El Capitan, the target of climbers from all over the world, also provides the cliffside aerie of one pair of falcons who accept, raise, and train the fledglings as their own, adding to the scant population. Climbers, so crucial in carrying out much of this special augmentation program, are also asked to keep well clear of the high-speed fliers whose skillful aerial acrobatics are often as thrilling to watch as their own.

Signs posted in Yosemite proclaim: "All Park animals are wild." It could be added that feeding animals is injurious to their health—and yours! In the 1970s, a child,

Top Left: Indian hemp in Leidig Meadow, Yosemite. Middle Left: Maple tree in bloom against a granite backdrop. Middle Right: Incense cedar at sunrise. Bottom Left: Ponderosa pine bark. Bottom Middle: Aspen trees in their fall colors. Bottom Right: Moonrise behind Jeffrey pine in Yosemite. Above: This protected peregrine falcon nests on the sheer face of El Capitan.

Above Left: Black bear are sometimes seen in Yosemite Valley, where they scrounge apples from the old, overgrown orchards near the Village. Above Right: Mule deer bucks crossing the Tuolumne River in the high country. Opposite: The call of the wild – a coyote howls amid the hushed snowy landscape of winter in Yosemite.

whose camera-aiming parents urged him to feed a deer, was accidentally killed by the antlered buck.

Many visitors want to view deer and bear in a natural setting. Unfortunately, most car-bound travelers can't see far beyond the edges of the road, and the last thing they want is to see a deer on the roadway itself. There is no doubt that the most rewarding way to observe wildlife is to hike along the many trails scattered throughout the Park. Observing the wildlife at a distance, however, is all that anyone should attempt.

Beware of Bears!

Viewing deer browsing in a meadow or leaping through the woods is an exciting, charming, and not uncommon sight. To see a bear ambling casually along or, better yet, shooing cubs up a tree is a far less likely event. Despite the actual color of their coats, Yosemite's bears are called black bear, *Ursus americanus,* and their lazy appearance belies formidable strength and power. Beware of bears.

Back in the unenlightened ages of the 1920s-1940s, the Park Service sponsored a nightly bear feeding program that was enjoyed by both mammals and humans. The "ohhing" and "ahhing" public was kept safely on one side of the river, the voracious bears, and an occasional skunk, on the other. They feasted on the "swell swill" trucked down from the kitchens of

The Ahwahnee Hotel while a ranger-naturalist explained the diners' native habits and habitats.

In 1937, the trained "garbage disposals" consumed as much as 60 tons of scraps per year! Biologists estimate that the natural food supply of Yosemite Valley can support fewer than 10 bears in the summer; during the palmy '30s, the population exploded to 60. Inevitably, of course, bears began breaking into buildings, cars, and camps causing property damage and personal injury.

Even though the unnatural, unhealthful feedings were discontinued in the early 1940s and various control programs instituted, including the destruction of 100 bears between 1960 and 1972, moochers continue to be a problem even today. Through a Human-Bear Management Program, bear-proof garbage cans and dumpsters have been installed in developed areas of the Park by the Curry Company and the Park Service. Bear-proof metal lockers have been placed in most campgrounds and some backcountry areas with a history of bear problems. Separating bears from human food and refuse has begun the process of returning the mammals to a natural state. One indication of the success of the program is the dramatic reduction in bear-caused injuries. Before installation of bear-proof containers, as many as 25 people were injured annually, a figure that has now

been reduced to one or two. Proper food storage is now a park regulation that protects both humans and bears.

As for the fabled grizzly bears, the last one in Yosemite was killed near Wawona in 1887. Their population, never large, was decimated by hunters in Yosemite and elsewhere in the state. As a consequence, grizzly bears no longer survive in the state of California.

Four-legged Bandits

Raccoons, with their crafty-looking, partly masked faces and ringed tails, are great opportunists and often seen, if not fed illegally, by visitors. Watch out, warns writer Sandy Dengler: "A raccoon will cheerfully bite the hand that feeds it." Its dexterity in climbing vertically, squeezing through small spaces, and manipulating garbage can lids qualify it as an ingenious little creature, but beware! A raccoon's disposition is far from admirable.

Coyotes are often spotted in meadows or alongside highways. Auto-killed squirrels are snatched soon after their death by an alert member of the coyote roadside patrols. Human food is equally popular with *Canis latrans,* which sometimes "sings" for its supper. Coyote howls, a characteristic of the once-wild West, are simultaneously traditional and yet unexpected—an echo from the past.

Cougars or mountain lions are definitely predatory, but they also perform a service, as their hunting rids the park of old and/or diseased deer. Smaller animals are consumed too, but venison on the hoof is the favored diet. Individual mountain lions follow herds of deer over many square miles; they are therefore constantly on the move and rarely seen. A cougar is a handsome figure, sleek, muscular, tawny in color with a ropelike tail—truly an outstanding mammal.

Squirrels are almost as numerous as Steller's jays and immensely popular with Park visitors, who are warned not to feed or touch them. They are far from an endangered species, but the ticks and fleas they carry can be harmful to people. High country marmots are another favorite.

Weasels, martens, foxes, bobcats, skunks, and other shier critters populate Yosemite, but they keep to byways not subject to casual observation.

Another isolationist mammal, treading the highest peaks and ridges, is the mountain bighorn sheep. Before 1900, these intrepid mountain climbers were high country dwellers and it is possible that their near-extinction was caused partly by domestic sheep, the "hoofed locusts," who transmitted ruin to high country meadows, and disease to the bighorn.

In March 1986, federal and state wildlife biologists moved a herd of 27 bighorns into Lee Vining Canyon below Tioga Pass in the expectation that they would eventually climb into Yosemite's high regions. They were free, but equipped with radio collars that emit signals so they could be monitored. Nine of the bighorns perished in late storms. By fall, seven more sheep had either wandered off or been killed, but nine lambs had been born so the herd had increased. Motorists on the Tioga Road were startled to see bighorns climbing the heights that year, and lambs were sighted through binoculars by biologists early in 1987.

Wildflowers Are Winners

No account of Yosemite's native inhabitants would be complete without mention of the vast array of spirit-lifting wildflowers that thrive here. From early spring, when baby blue eyes, goldfields, and poppies carpet the slopes of the Merced River Canyon, till the last bloom of rabbit-brush and goldenrod in the high country, Yosemite enjoys a profuse procession of some 1,400 flowers. Various species of lupine, yarrow, Mariposa lilies, farewell-to-spring, pussy paws, fireweed, and penstemon create colorful borders along roads. Rarer blooms, such as monkshood, Sierra primrose, snowplants, and sky pilot can be discovered in more secluded spots off the beaten road and path.

Wherever blooms are found, they lift the heart as does all the natural beauty and wildlife of Yosemite National Park. The good news continues to be that there is still an unspoiled place where nature reigns supreme.

Hidden Yosemite

Above: Maple leaves and granite. Below: A solitary hiker in the Valley. Right: Moonset in Yosemite Valley.

*E*ven on a busy holiday weekend in Yosemite Valley when traffic is heavy and campgrounds are full, it is possible to be alone. How? Park your mechanical beetle and walk, or ride a bike, away from the visitor complex. Within five minutes you can be alone in some piney nook, rock-sheltered cranny, or forest-encircled meadow. Hidden Yosemite is never very far away.

Sightseers by the hundreds make the pilgrimage to Glacier Point to "ooh" and "ahh" at the spectacular vistas below, and sweeping away right and left, beyond its 7,214-foot height. Nearby boulders, trees, and grassy hollows offer retreat, and trails lead away into quiet woods.

As the hub of the high country, Tuolumne Meadows features a Visitor Center, gas station, mountaineering center, tent store, camps, and stables. Beyond those facilities lies a grassy, river-threaded landscape where many a haven restores the weariest soul. Backpackers plod the beaten trails, but within minutes of even the most popular trail, such as the John Muir Trail, you can be alone with breeze, beauty, and solitude. Similar seclusion and escapes from civilization can be sought and found within minutes of Tioga Pass, where hundreds of autos and passengers enter Yosemite daily.

Although reached by a side road and off the beaten path, White Wolf is a popular destination due to its lodge, tent camp, large public campground, and stables, but again, a "hidden" Yosemite is within a short distance of the facilities. Wawona, on the south side of the Park, is a popular year-round resort, but there are peaceful retreats aplenty close by on the fringes of the golf course or in the forest behind the hotel. During the summer, a stunning array of wildflowers animates the meadows of the Badger Pass ski area where skiers swoop and streak each winter. More sedate cross-country skiers find solitude in the adjacent snow-shrouded forest along hundreds of miles of trails.

Trams carry sightseers through the magnificent Mariposa Grove of giant sequoias, but walkers find an awesome silence and sense of isolation on trails through the massive and mysterious forest. There is a feeling of space and the infinite richness of the Earth. Experienced backpackers seek the less-traveled trails and in this way can be alone for days at a time, but they rarely reveal the location to others for fear of discovery. For the inexperienced visitor who craves space and needs nature's peace, the "stay on designated trails" advice appears restrictive. But along the 700 miles of park trails there beckon many small standpoints of silence—islands of repose away from mainstream Yosemite.

Above: Frost-covered grass on Yosemite Valley floor. Right: An unusual view of Yosemite Falls with Merced River in the foreground.

Yosemite and the Imagination

Above: A guide in the Yosemite backcountry points to Indian pictographs on the rock. Photograph by Ansel Adams. Right: Yosemite Valley (El Capitan and Bridalveil Fall), 1876, by Thomas Hill.

Beginning in July 1855, when author James Hutchings and artist Thomas Ayres attempted to depict Yosemite Valley's incredible scenery, writers, painters, and photographers have stretched their imaginations to interpret a place that defies credibility. Writers have been so prolific that the Yosemite Research Library boasts a large collection of more than 500 books focusing on the Park's history, flora, fauna, and inhabitants—both real and imaginary. They range from the sublime, Muir's *My First Summer in the Sierra,* to the ludicrous *Forked Lightning,* a novel correctly subtitled *A Wild Tale of the Yosemite Valley.*

Hundreds of travel books containing everything from a casual mention to several detailed chapters about Yosemite make collecting a library of books on Yosemite a never-ending pursuit. Diversity reigns, from straight-forward praise by Helen Hunt Jackson to oblique references by Gertrude Stein and Thomas Wolfe. Hutchings was practical, yet rhapsodic, notably in his 1886 *In the Heart of the Sierras* Galen Clark, aged, earnest, and pedestrian, wrote three slim volumes at the turn of the century. Of the pioneer authors, John Muir was by far the most poetic. At least two more authors who successfully combined imagination with information to produce classic books, were Clarence King in his 1872 *Mountaineering in the Sierra Nevada,* and J. Smeaton Chase in his 1911 *Yosemite Trails.*

Bards and Beauty

Poets are expected to be imaginative, but most 19th century poets produced little more than rhymed reverence. Jean Bruce Washburn, the matriach of Wawona culture from 1874 until the early 1900s, equated Yosemite with Paradise on Earth. God wrought the natural wonders, she wrote, "that lift the mind in high and sacred thought."

All poets, from traditional to contemporary, have stretched their imagination and vocabulary to portray the marvelous mountains of Yosemite. None, in this writer's opinion, have succeeded as well as non-poet John Muir. One of his prose poems, published years later in *My First Summer in the Sierra,* was his journal entry for June 23, 1869:

> *…Nevermore, however weary, should one faint by the way who gains the blessings of one mountain day; whatever his fate, long life, short life, stormy or calm, he is rich forever.*

The Inner Eye

Documentation exists in caves and on cliffs that Thomas Ayres, in 1855, was not the first artist in Yosemite. Eons before that 1855 date, Indian people contributed art with their pictographs. These ancient, rarely-seen rock paintings exhibit a primitive, predominantly linear design, achieved with red, orange, gray, and white paint. Their meaning is not known, but Jim Snyder, an expert on Indian culture, estimates that the hun-

Above Left: Thomas Hill. Above Right: Valley scene by William Keith.

dreds of drawings relate specifically to social and economic life, "possibly guides to game trails or favored hunting spots, and records of weather or trade." Because of their uniqueness and fragility, the location of pictographs is not publicized.

Although confined to specific traditional rules, Indian women expressed great creativity in the design, shape, size, and quality of their utilitarian baskets and cradleboards. Later, according to Yosemite's curator of ethnography, Craig Bates, "new basket forms were designed, and new materials, such as glass beads, thread and yarn, were incorporated into native arts in response to tourist demands."

Thomas Ayres, however, was the forerunner of many, non-native American artists of national and even worldwide renown to visit Yosemite. Albert Bierstadt, William Keith, Thomas Hill, Virgil Williams, Chris Jorgensen, Herman Herzog, Thomas Moran, William Hahn, and Lady Constance Gordon-Cumming were among the prestigious artists who tried to capture the essence of Yosemite on canvas. Their paintings relfected an intriguing and divergent vision.

In the mid-19th century, Albert Bierstadt was celebrated as a master with a paintbrush, but sometimes his vivid colors and waterfalls cascading from the sky were considered exercises in wild blue imagination. One surprising critic was Mark Twain, no stranger to hyperbole himself, who complained, "We do not want this glorified atmosphere smuggled into a portrait of Yosemite, where it surely does not belong…this atmosphere of Mr. Bierstadt's is altogether too gorgeous." If Twain could see the vibrant splashes of color used by contemporary artists, he would realize that Bierstadt's work could almost be termed "avant-garde." Bierstadt's romanticized paintings are now treasured by more than 90 art museums and galleries.

Several of the legion of famed landscape artists who visited Yosemite in the late 1800s were so inspired they stayed on for months or even years. In 1878, after one look at what she described as an "extraordinary combination of granite crags and stupendous waterfalls," Lady Gordon-Cumming cancelled her stage departure. Instead of three days, she remained in the Valley for three months, making 25 drawings and 50 watercolors by day, and writing lively, literate letters to her family in Scotland at night. Later, that correspondence was published in her excellent book, *Granite Crags*. Both the book and her charming pictures are now prized.

Lady Gordon-Cumming's residence was transitory in comparison to those of Thomas Hill and Charles Dorman Robinson. Hill's first visit was in 1863, but from 1886 until his death in 1908, he was a gregarious, brush-wielding, cigar-chomping, seasonal fixture at the Wawona Hotel. His tenure at the hotel was assured due to his fame and because one of his daughters had married one of the owners, John Wash-

A Scene of Indian life by Constance Gordon-Cumming (top). Chris Jorgensen (above right) was a popular Yosemite artist. Shown here are his paintings of Indian granaries (top right) and sequoia trees (above middle). B. Laycock's painting of Yosemite Valley shows a very different style (above left).

Yosemite Valley, 1868, *by Albert Bierstadt.*

Above: Chris Jorgensen's hitherto unpublished portrait of Galen Clark at 90.

yet sold many paintings. His mammoth 50- by 380-foot panorama of Yosemite Valley, so detailed as to be mind-boggling, was exhibited in Paris. Soon after Robinson left the Valley, Chris Jorgensen and Harry Cassie Best took up residence. The former stayed for 19 summers, the latter 35.

Like Hill, under whom he had studied, Norwegian-born Chris Jorgensen was convivial, and a prodigious worker who enjoyed patronage from hotel guests. His rustic and picturesque home on the Merced River near the Sentinel Hotel was a mecca for tourists and residents. He and his wife Angela Ghirardelli Jorgensen were wholeheartedly involved in the community. Among their friends was aged, poverty-stricken, ex-guardian Galen Clark. They contributed several drawings of Indian life to the pioneer's slim book on Yosemite's original inhabitants, and Jorgensen, who rarely made portraits, painted one of Clark.

Today, the artist is best known for his wonderful watercolors of the California Missions, Monterey Peninsula, and his Yosemite pictures, which are highly valued by collectors. Yosemite National Park, the Bancroft Library, the Huntington Library, and the Los Angeles County Museum of Natural History are major repositories of his work. Jorgensen's biographer, Dr. Katherine M. Littell, owns the largest private collection of his paintings.

In 1902, four years after Jorgensen became Yosemite's artist-in-residence, Canadian Harry Best offered some competition by opening Best's Studio, where his paintings were for sale. His penchant for dark colors resulted in less popular pictures, but his generous disposition won him a host of friends. Best's marriage to Anne Rippey in 1901 was celebrated within the spray of Bridalveil Fall; 27 years later their daughter Virginia participated in another notable Yosemite marriage. As it was winter, the ceremony took place in Best's Studio. The bridegroom was a young photographer named Ansel Adams.

During the 1920s, Yosemite had two more notable artists-in-residence, although Swedish native Gunnar

burn. A separate studio was built for Hill, which guests loved to visit not only to meet a real artist and view his works, but to see the curios he collected. Everything from rattlesnake skins and rattles to bearskins, baskets, deer antlers, arrowheads and, of course, paintings adorned the studio. Today it is maintained seasonally in similar fashion by the National Park Service.

Hill's classic works, combining realism with a dreamy focus on light, sold readily to guests from all over the world. President Theodore Roosevelt took a complimentary painting home to the White House after a quick 1903 tour of the studio. John Muir paid $500 for a Hill landscape of the Muir Glacier in Alaska. That and several other enormous landscapes are on display in the Oakland Museum, and the state capital of California, Sacramento.

Robinson, who spent many summers in the Valley, was less successful, and far less congenial than his contemporary, Hill,

Above: Harry Cassie Best, artist, owner of Best's Studio, and father-in-law of Ansel Adams.
Left: Yosemite Valley from Inspiration Point *by Harry Cassie Best.*

"Weedy" Widforss spent half his time at Grand Canyon. He specialized in realistic watercolors that were monumental yet intimate. A dozen of his splendid scenes hang in the entrance lobby of The Ahwahnee, and yet another is reproduced as the cover of the Hotel's dinner menu.

One of "Weedy's" local fans was Della Taylor Hoss who, as wife of a Curry Co. executive, lived in the Valley from 1925 to 1942. She specialized in depicting trees, and published her meticulously executed tree-and-cone linocuts as illustrations in Mary Curry Tressider's *The Trees of Yosemite*, first printed in 1931. When *Discovering Sierra Trees* was published by the Yosemite Natural History Association in 1973, with imaginative yet realistic black-and-white illustrations by Jane Gyer, Della Hoss was one of the first to offer congratulations. Later, the book won the first National Park Service Director's Award.

Mrs. Gyer, whose Yosemite affiliation began in 1956, said, "I have no background; I paint my feelings," but she has studied in Europe and the Orient, as well as America. Her watercolors are much sought out by those who are glad that she continues to be "dedicated to the task of visually interpreting this [Yosemite's] drama."

Paintings by Gunnar Widforss (shown painting in Yosemite) were used as souvenir menu covers at The Ahwahnee, where several of his paintings hang in the lobby.

Le Conte Fall on the Tuolumne river in Yosemite.

Although Yosemite was a focal point for pioneer photographers, in the early years their pursuit of just the right picture was complicated by cumbersome equipment and the need for a string of pack mules to haul it. At least two cameras were essential: a double-lens stereoscopic camera, which was relatively lightweight, and a "box" camera, which weighed close to 40 pounds, for panoramic views. Until the late 1870s, "film" was non-existent, so glass plates, weighing up to a pound each, had to be carried. Once a vantage point had been selected, and the camera set on a wooden tripod, the photographer had to duck into a "darkroom," usually an enclosed buggy or tent, to carefully immerse the plate with chemicals before sensitizing it to light with silver nitrate. After it was exposed briefly in the camera, the fragile plate had to be returned to darkness for development.

Considering the need for speed and efficiency required for developing, compounded by the problems caused by wind, dust, and lack of water, it's amazing that so many photographs turned out as well as they did. Had equipment been easier to handle, Charles L. Weed, Yosemite's first photographer, might have achieved less ordinary views in 1859. Two years later, Carleton E. Watkins arrived burdened with a specially-designed mammoth camera that held 18- by 22-inch plates. His lightest, but most important, equipment was his eye for composition. It was almost as revolutionary in scope as the huge camera he used. Besides meriting wide sales and awards, his photographs helped convince U.S. Congressmen to preserve the irreplaceable scenic wonders of the Valley by voting for the Yosemite Grant Act in 1864.

Edweard J. Muybridge was the next master photographer to capture the cliffs, domes, and river of the Valley in prints and stereos. If nature wasn't grand enough to suit him, he rearranged it by chopping intrusive branches, or whole trees, with no thought of environmental impact. Seemingly, Muybridge was as indestructible as he was indefatigable. Once, in his quest for spectacular pictures, he had himself lowered by ropes into the depths of the Valley. His off-camera adventures, including the murder of his wife's lover, made him as famed as his photos; (a jury judged him innocent by reason of insanity).

In 1872, Muybridge made 11 haunting stereos depicting Yosemite Indians, their camps, and already disappearing lifestyle. Artist Albert Bierstadt had commissioned the views, but Muybridge's inquisitive eye and way with people captured the reality of what contemporary photographer Ted Orland terms "people living in intimate relationship with the land."

Of the numerous photographers who frequented Yosemite, four who rooted themselves in the Valley for years deserve special mention. George Fiske, a bearded and rotund fixture from the early 1870s until his death in 1918, specialized in splendid winter scenes. His friend Galen Clark was a favorite subject, posed by the Wawona Tunnel Tree, or standing nonchalantly atop a pile of snow on the jutting Overhanging Rock at Glacier Point.

Two men vied to be Fiske's commercial and artistic successor: Arthur C. Pillsbury, whose expanded services included a motion picture theater, may have been the financial heir, but during his 1900-1939 tenure, Julius T. Boysen was more of an artistic heir. He took the usual views of natural features with graphic clarity, but also concentrated on small objects including wildflowers and animals. His views of deer, reproduced on postcards, appear uniquely natural, and those of bears were perennial bestsellers. One of Boysen's specialties was the making of sensitive portraits of the local Indians.

By the late 1920s, Boysen and all other photographers had a competitor who excelled in his knowledge of everything from the piano keyboard to lenses, filters, cameras, and finally the printing of masterpiece prints. Ansel Adams' equipment was always first-rate, but by far his greatest asset was his creative vision. Adams' inspiration was backed by meticulous study, experimentation, and developing of fine prints. Eventually, he could afford to

Top: George Fiske made a good living as a commercial photographer in Yosemite in the 1870s. Above: J.T. Boysen's Studio was next to the general store in Yosemite Village.

Baby blue eyes. Photograph by Dana Morgenson.

break away from commercial photography, becoming instead a purist, creating new appreciation for photography as art. He believed that experience expanded art, and said, "The role of an artist in the environment is a complex pattern of adjustment between the objective and subjective, the informative and the enlightening." Incidentally, the reason the word "photo" does not appear in this book is because Ansel Adams detested it as a demeaning term. His death in 1984 may have ended his career, but his work will surely live forever. Today, legions of photographers, influenced by Adams' work, teaching, and his lectures on photography, keep his spirit alive in their own work.

In contrast with Adams' preference for black and white film, in the use of which he was a master, most contemporary photographers opt for color. The results are uneven, but imaginative men and women, such as Dana Morgenson, in particular, have found great personal expression through color photography, much of which appeared in his SRO slide shows, popular books, and postcards. Morgenson's eloquence extended far beyond the camera for, as the Curry Company Director of Guest Activities, his gentle voice and guidance made him a veritable Pied Piper on his daily Camera Walks. In addition, his seasonal newsletters were anticipated

and often saved by 7,500 eager recipients. Morgenson's death in 1980 ended 32 years of residency in Yosemite, but his personal impact, pictures, and books survive, as does the Dana and Esther Morgenson Trail outside The Ahwahnee Hotel. In an accolade that fit himself as well as Dana Morgenson, Ansel Adams wrote, "His gentle persuasion opened doors of vision and comprehension."

Today, there are many talented photographers following in Adams' footsteps, and in recent years, motion picture filmmaking in Yosemite has come of artistic age. The National Geographic Society has applauded Bob Roney's *Yosemite and the High Sierra* nature film, and another spectacular movie is *Yosemite Climbing* by Peter Kern, a Swiss, who portrays the majesty, thrill, and excitement of climbing. Two other documentary films, one on John Muir, the other on Ansel Adams, are already classics.

Pageants, notably the Bracebridge Dinner at Christmas, and plays have long been a popular art form in the Park. Actor Lee Stetson has also made a major individual contribution. Beginning in 1983, when he first presented his authentic and inspirational "An Evening with John Muir," Stetson's engrossing presentations have drawn appreciative crowds in Yosemite Valley, as well as on national stages.

The Flourishing Arts in Yosemite

*L*ook at my painting! It's terrible, but I did it myself." That type of comment from adults and children is often voiced at the end of a free art lesson in Yosemite Valley. Whether decorative or daub, winning or wild, the I-did-it-myself pictures are an expression of creativity, an interpretation of nature, and proof that art is alive and well in Yosemite. Pictographs are no longer made, but line drawings and prints are. Stereoptician views are no longer taken, but still lifes and three-dimensional images in black and white or living color are.

Hub of much of the amateur output is the Yosemite Art Activity Center on the Mall immediately west of the main post office in Yosemite Valley. Fittingly, it is housed in J.T. Boysen's former photography studio. From approximately May 1 to mid-October, art classes without charge are offered between 10:00 a.m. and 2:00 p.m. daily. There is no age limit, but children under 12 need to be accompanied by an adult. Although personal achievement and informality are the keynote of the sessions, the instructors are reputable professionals who are happy teaching and painting amid the ever-changing challenge of Yosemite's varied splendor.

The Center, where art and photographic supplies, books, posters, etc. can be purchased, was founded in 1983 "to motivate artists to develop diverse interpretations of Yosemite and varied landscapes." The Art Activity Center is financed by sales, and more significantly, by the Yosemite Park and Curry Co., the Yosemite Association, and the National Park Service.

In 1985, the Yosemite Renaissance Art Exhibit was initiated by local artists and sponsored by the Yosemite Park and Curry Co., the National Park Service, Mariposa County Arts Council, and the Yosemite Natural History Association. Though the program is held on intermittent years, it was successful in that it created and fos-

Learning how to take a nature photograph in Yosemite Valley.

tered the environment for artists to re-interpret Yosemite in a current and contemporary light.

The National Park Service arranges exhibits in the Visitor Center in the Valley, and also sponsors an artist-in-residence program.

Occasionally, free photography classes are offered by the Art Activity Center, but serious students eagerly pay tuition next door at the Ansel Adams Gallery for one of its twice-yearly workshops. Begun in 1942, these workshops are demanding, exhausting, and exhilarating. Each session matches master landscape with master instructors who trained under the master himself.

Extensive programs that explore appreciation of photography, wine, fine cooking, musical theater, and opera are conducted by the Curry Company from November through March. Their "Yosemite Holidays" series has received critical acclaim for its unique programs. In addition, the Yosemite Association offers professional weekend seminars in photography, writing and poetry, natural and human history, for a fee.

Whether a person is skilled or unskilled, Yosemite National Park evokes creativity by inspiring visitors to express themselves with everything from native plants to yarn, pen, pencil, brush, camera, and even tape recorder. The universal aim is to capture something of the essence of magnificent Yosemite.

Ansel Adams:
Illuminating an "Environment of Majesty"

*Above: Ansel Adams in the 1980s.
Right: Ski joring in Yosemite
Valley in the Thirties. Photograph
by Ansel Adams.*

Shortly after Ansel Adams' death in 1984 at the age of 82, a *Sacramento Bee* cartoonist pictured him arriving in heaven. "Follow me, Ansel," St. Peter said, "We've got a view of Yosemite Valley that nobody has ever photographed!"

For 68 years, the expansive, bearded man meticulously photographed Yosemite and the West, at all hours and in all seasons, ever striving, whether afield or in a darkroom, to produce the perfect image and finest print. In the fullest sense of the word, he was an artist. In addition to that skill, Ansel Adams was a pianist, writer, teacher, actor, producer, and conservationist, or as he styled himself, a "constructive belligerent."

Ansel's hyperactive and unconventional boyhood on the then western fringe of San Francisco was dominated by nature, the nearby ocean, and two contrasting instruments of artistic expression. The first, which he began mastering at the age of 12, was a piano, the second was a box camera that was given to him on his first visit to Yosemite in 1916. Ansel, a reedy, dark-haired sprite, was instantly intoxicated with Yosemite's splendor and set about attempting to mirror its beauties with the Kodak camera. From then on the Park was a magnet and obsession.

During the summers of 1920 and 1921, he was custodian of the Sierra Club Lodge in Yosemite Valley, but had ample time to explore the High Sierra, which he termed "an environment of majesty." His camera accompanied him, but a career as a concert pianist was his major goal. Daily practice was imperative and, in 1921, he was invited by Harry C. Best, proprietor of Best's Studio in Yosemite Valley, to use his piano. This delighted Ansel, then 19, and he soon recognized a kindred spirit in Best's 17-year-old daughter Virginia. Due to their youth and his unremunerative ambition, they were not married until 1928. By then, Ansel was a vital even boisterous part of the Yosemite community, and had estab-

lished what he called a "minimal" reputation as a photographer. Don Tresidder, president of the newly formed Yosemite Park and Curry Co., hired him to take publicity pictures in the Park at $10.00 a day plus expenses for three months a year. For the next decade, this part-time job added to his reputation as a landscape artist and helped support his family during the Depression. Virginia aided her father in Best's Studio and cared for their children, Michael and Anne.

Music remained integral to their lives, but Ansel was finally committed to photography as a profession. His favorite subjects were natural—trees, mountains, clouds—but his need for daily bread forced him to take advertising shots of commercial items ranging from hotels to a loaf of bread. No matter what the assigned subject, he did his best to take, and print, a technically excellent picture.

Ansel's output promoting tourism to Yosemite was reproduced on menus and postcards, and in albums, books, and magazines. His reputation grew, and as it did, he moved from supporting himself by taking advertising and publicity photographs, to sustaining himself and his family by selling artistic works. Much of the boost given his career resulted from the exposure he obtained from his photographs being exhibited and sold to hotel guests at the park.

Although Ansel terminated his photographic work for the Curry Company in 1938, his involvement with Yosemite continued, partly because Best's Studio was managed by his wife after her father's death. That concession operates now as the Ansel Adams Gallery under the direction of his son and daughter-in-law.

Ansel's commercial and artistic work took him far afield. Increasingly, his landscapes were exhibited and sold nationally. Furthermore, they influenced the conservation movement, particularly with the publication of a portfolio that helped per-

suade Congress to establish King's Canyon National Park. Honors and awards, including the Medal of Freedom, were given him, and usually placed on what he called his "ego wall." Neither recognition nor wealth diverted him from his quest for excellence in subject and printmaking. Perfection was ever a goal, retirement never. Not even a heart bypass stopped him from teaching and lecturing all over the country.

Throughout his life, Ansel devoted himself to bestowing knowledge, joy, inspiration, and pleasure to all through his photographs, leadership in conservation issues, and his magnetic personality. His heart and soul were never far from the high country of Yosemite where Mt. Ansel Adams, as rugged and uncompromising as he, was dedicated to his memory in 1985.

The Yosemite Park and Curry Co.

Above: David Curry calling Curry campers to breakfast. Right: Jennie and David Curry at Camp Curry, with Jennie's father, Robert Foster, circa 1904.

I t is now 7:30 in the morning; those who do not rise for breakfast by 8:00 a.m. will have to postpone it till tomorrow," the booming call resounded through the pines and tents at Camp Curry before rising to an echoing crescendo. "At eight o'clock the cook gets HOT AND BURNS THE BREAKFAST!" For years, guests were awakened and hurried along by David Curry's stentorian admonition, and sent off to bed by his equally sonorous nightly benediction of "ALL'S WELL!"

All was not well when the camp welcomed its first nine guests on June 1, 1899. No one in Yosemite Valley, not even kindly Galen Clark, who felt that the site near the base of Glacier Point was too cold and isolated, forecast anything but financial doom for the innovative enterprise. No one could foresee that it would outlast all established concessions and, by the late 1980s, would be well on its way to celebrating its first 100 years.

Of the 4,500 people who visited Yosemite in 1899, John D. Rockefeller, William Jennings Bryan, and many others paid a minimum of $4 a day to stay at the Sentinel Hotel, by then the only one left of several pioneer hotels in the Valley. There, linen tablecloths, live (but muted) background dinner music, and tipping prevailed. Less affluent visitors camped out in one of the Valley's public campgrounds, where scenery compensated for lack of even rudimentary conveniences.

During that summer, a total of 290 people stayed at Curry's new inconspicuous camp where for $2 a day they enjoyed beds under a canvas roof, three square meals a day, and a clean napkin every meal! Tipping was not allowed. A small staff of college students worked for their board and a cot-in-the-rocks; one cook was paid $100 for the season. Managers Jennie and David Curry greeted each guest in a friendly but not deferential way. Camp Curry was almost a revolutionary concept. By the end of the summer, there were 25 tents, used by an average of only three and one-third guests per night. Fortunately, most guests stayed at least a week. Residents persisted, however, in saying that the upstart camp would never last.

Mother and Dad Curry

Neither of its managers, barrel-chested, bombastic David A. Curry or his gentle, frail-appearing wife Jennie Foster Curry, was daunted by the doomsayers. Both were born-and-bred Hoosiers, graduates of Indiana University, whose school-teaching careers had led them to Northern California. They were also highly moral—adamantly opposed to smoking, drinking, and unchaperoned mingling of young people. Their attitude was characteristic of the times. Both were motivated by public service. Camp guests, they felt, should be considered as if they were family. Their strengths were complementary. "Dad" Curry was a born showman who used his booming voice to entertain; "Mother" Curry was the organizer whose quiet tone conveyed authority. He established popular calls and traditions, possessed the muscle to move boulders and erect tents, and

Top: Camp Curry guests had tents, three square meals a day, and clean napkins every meal. Above: The cedar tree in the sitting room of James Hutchings' Cedar Cottage, which was eventually replaced by the new Ahwahnee Hotel. Stereograph by B.L. Singley, circa 1899. Right: The nightly Firefall provided a spectacle for visitors in the Valley until 1968.

had the brains to do the bookkeeping and long-range planning. Mother Curry directed the ordering, preparation, and serving of meals, the washing of all those napkins, and other essential behind-the-scenes operations. If needed, she could make salads, bake bread, wait tables, or help put up tents, and none of these tasks, she said, "hurt my pride." It was David who established the nightly entertainments, fought for concessions with Goliath, in the person of Army Superintendents, and astounded guests with his computer-like memory. It was the Stentor, as he liked to be known, who reestablished the Firefall from atop Glacier Point and made it a must-see nightly ceremony, but it was Mother Curry who saw that each tent was supplied with candles and extra blankets. She was the one who interviewed, counseled, and comforted the predominantly youthful staff, but he was the one to lend them money.

After her husband died of blood poisoning in 1917, Mother Curry proved that she, too, was a shrewd businessperson. When she discovered that the porters were receiving sizable tips, she cut their salaries from $90 to $75 a month. Nevertheless, the staff respected and loved her because of her fairness and her willingness to pitch in when they were shorthanded. Her own children, Foster, Marjorie, and Mary, worked their way up from menial to managerial jobs in the family business. By 1925, 100 different positions were offered at Camp Curry. "A desire to spend the summer in Yosemite is not sufficient qualification for a position," she warned on application forms. "If you cannot make a bed, sweep a room, and care for a bathroom exquisitely, do not apply as maids. If you are not willing to keep the grounds clean, empty the slopjars, and 'rustle' the baggage, do not apply as porter."

Success

Within a decade of Camp Curry's establishment, three rival camps were set up, showing that other concessionaires had the message that campers preferred informal, low-cost accommodations to roughing it. By 1925, the National Park Service tired of the incessant battling of competing businesses and forced a merger, which was negotiated by Horace Albright. The outcome was the formation of the Yosemite Park and Curry Co., led by charismatic Donald B. Tresidder, who had married the bosses' daughter Mary. Mother Curry must have thought it ironic that building a luxury hotel to replace the decrepit Sentinel was one of the terms in the new contract with the Park Service.

Don Tresidder, who had shot up from porter to president in 11 years, switched his allegiance from the camp to the operation of the Yosemite Park and Curry Co. His responsibilities included the 71-room Sentinel Hotel; the youthful 90-room Glacier Point Hotel; the 14-room Big Trees Lodge in the Mariposa Grove; Yosemite Lodge, which had pillows enough for 1,260 guests; six High Sierra camps, where the early day atmosphere of Camp Curry prevailed; the general store; and such accessory services as stables, a laundry, and a print shop. His most challenging job was to oversee the building of an outstanding yet environmentally unobtrusive hotel. It was to be called The Ahwahnee.

Above: Sweet-faced Jennie ("Mother") Curry. Below: A youthful Donald B. Tresidder and Mary Curry Tresidder. In 1925, Don Tresidder became the first president of the newly formed Yosemite Park and Curry Co.

Top: Construction of The Ahwahnee Hotel was completed in July 1927. Above: (Left to right) Park Superintendent W.B. Lewis, A.B.C. Dohrmann, Tom Vint, Don Tresidder, and architect Gilbert Stanley Underwood proudly display the architectural plan for The Ahwahnee. Right: Ansel Adams' photographs of The Ahwahnee Hotel (clockwise from top): the exterior, the huge fireplace in the Great Lounge, and one of the magnificent floor-to-ceiling windows in the same room.

Luxury

Construction of the six-floor, 100-room, roughly Y-shaped building began on April 1, 1926, and despite problems with personalities, delays, and supplies, it opened 15 months later. An obsolete stables complex was removed on the northeast side of the Valley to make room for the rock-and-steel structure that merged rather than conflicted with the cliffs. An enormous dining room with a seating capacity of 350 exhibited rustic architecture, while the 77-foot long, 51-foot wide Great Lounge with its 23-foot high ceiling, was in grander style. Traces of Art Deco were subordinate to the charming and unique Native-American ornamentation, which prevails throughout the hotel.

In contrast with Camp Curry, and its can't-tell-the-help-from-the-guests atmosphere, formality dominated at The Ahwahnee. Uniformed employees included a shoeshine boy and a forbidding doorman who disdainfully stopped anyone so vulgar as to seek entrance without a coat and tie. Park Service Director Stephen Mather was delighted with everything from the Persian rugs, stained glass windows, lofty ceilings, murals, handwoven bedspreads and rugs, to pewter inkstands, elaborate meals, and the large deferential staff. The hoi polloi could camp or stay at Camp Curry at a maximum of $4.50 a night, but those with prestige and/or money could register at The Ahwahnee for rooms costing from $15 to $50 a day.

The irony of unbridled luxury in a national park did not faze Mather, who had known wealth from birth, yet at least one critic compared the hotel to a millionaire's palace, and said, "It causes the restless to be more restless."

Retrenching

Before long, too many specialty chefs, an oversized staff, and too few guests spoiled the financial broth and caused Curry executives to rethink their approach. By 1928, staff and costs were cut, but seven guest cottages and two tennis courts were constructed. The stock market crash of 1929 and the ensuing Depression terminated "unbridled luxury" at the hotel and nearly forced the Company into bankruptcy. During 1933, only 296,000 people visited Yosemite, and the Company's profit was reduced to $1,495!

It was 1936 before the national economy improved enough so that visitation topped 400,000 again. Even then, there were more empty than occupied rooms at The Ahwahnee. During a disastrous flood in December 1937, a mere five guests rattled around in the hotel.

Yosemite at War

World War II was the next major event to affect national and local economy. Gas rationing decreased Park visitation to 127,643 people in 1943, and 119,515 in 1944. Many Yosemite residents joined the Armed Services, others left to work in war industries, and the remaining bare-bones population raised Victory gardens as well as money for war bonds and the Red Cross. Incongruously, military units trained amid peaceful, sylvan scenes at Wawona, but not even that was enough. Uncle Sam, in the guise of the U.S. Navy, commandeered The Ahwahnee as a special hospital. Instead of a few, decorous guests reading or talking quietly in the Great Lounge, 350 battle-weary sailors slept in rows of double-decked bunks in Ward A. Even without carpets or drapes, the converted dining room was a classy mess hall. The Sweet Shop was transformed into a commissary, the bar became a chapel, and the Tresidders' sixth-floor suite was used by the commanding officer.

Perhaps the sailors appreciated the grand setting and sublime views, but the bulk of the men stationed in The Ahwahnee wanted to be on the high seas or, failing that, desired girls and beer to help speed their convalescence. "Yosemite," groused one "white hat," "is a beautiful place surrounded by solitude!"

Although the Navy evacuated by January 1946, it was the following Christmas before guests could be welcomed once more. But the high living of the 1920s never returned. Today, The Ahwahnee is still a grand and classic hotel, but it is enjoyed by everyone from casually dressed non-

Above: Stephen Mather with model of the planned Yosemite Village. Right (clockwise from top): The outdoor ice rink at Camp Curry in the 1930s. Ice skating at the rink is still a popular winter activity. During World War II, the U.S. Navy commandeered The Ahwahnee as a special hospital for recuperating sailors. The Wawona Hotel is located 25 miles south of the Valley.

guests to formally attired VIPs and visiting royalty such as Queen Elizabeth II and Prince Philip of England.

Mother Curry's Reign

Until her death in 1948, Mother Curry felt sorry for the "poor dears" who stayed at Yosemite Lodge or The Ahwahnee and refused to spend more than a few hours at the hotel. Her official reign at Camp Curry ended in 1936 when, at aged 71, she turned its management over to daughter Mary Curry Tresidder, but her behind-the-scenes influence was far from over. Before she died in her beloved bungalow two days short of 87, she had participated in the Camp's 50th anniversary, and had the pleasure of seeing two grandsons—David and John Curry—working at the Camp. They were astounded to witness their kindly "Nana" in the no-nonsense managerial role that earned her obedience, respect, and awe from the staff. The teenagers' jobs were lowly with the sole exception of David's nightly nightmare of calling for the Firefall. "I inherited my grandfather's name," he said later, "but not his vocal powers."

The Lodge

Yosemite Lodge is the third major guest unit in Yosemite Valley. It was established in 1915 as a competitor to Camp Curry, with 156 tents in contrast to the seven the Currys had boasted in 1899. D.J. Desmond, the concessionaire, had leased the site of the former Cavalry camp. The troopers' tents became guest lodging, the barracks were remodeled into a lounge and dining room, and the bath houses spruced up to meet guest needs. Yosemite Falls Camp, as it was known for a few years, was an instant success. Later, the Desmond enterprise was merged with the newly formed Yosemite Park and Curry Co., and cabins replaced the tents. At present, Yosemite Lodge is open all year round and can sleep more than 1,500 guests in its 485 motel-type units and cabins. The converted barracks were replaced years ago by an attractive, sprawling building that houses a cafeteria, the Four Seasons restaurant, and the Mountain Room Broiler.

Farewell, Currys

Until the late 1970s, the Curry family was still associated with the Park (a Curry great-granddaughter waited tables in one of the restaurants), but their tenure had effectively ended with Mary Curry Tresidder's death in her sixth-floor Ahwahnee suite in October 1970. Three years later, MCA purchased the company following short-term ownership and management by Shasta Telecasting Corp. and then U.S. Natural Resources. Under the successful leadership of Edward C. Hardy, its president, the Yosemite Park and Curry Co. has retained its historic name as well as the strong commitment to service and hospitality that was the hallmark of Jennie and David Curry.

Hardy's position is more complex than that of any preceding Company president. Under the Park Service policy of having one primary concessionaire to operate all the major guest facilities in a given park, the Curry Company operates all of the hotels, tent camps, grocery stores, gas stations, gift shops, stables, restaurants, and other facilities deemed appropriate by the National Park Service, which oversees the company's operations. A few exceptions are the Yosemite Medical Clinic, the U.S. Post Office, the Yosemite Institute, and the Ansel Adams Gallery, which are independent concessionaires.

Since 1932, the five-unit, 105-room Wawona Hotel has been under Curry management, as has Degnan's delicatessen and restaurant since 1974. Concessions are run by the chief concessionaire under a long-term contract for which the Yosemite Park and Curry Co. pays a percentage of revenue determined by the United States Government. Thus, the Company, its services, and rates are controlled by the National Park Service. No price change or structural improvement can be made without the approval of the NPS. Its superintendent, protective, and interpretive divisions are mandated by the U.S. Congress.

The Magic of Bracebridge

Above: A jester entertains at the Bracebridge Dinner. Below: Squire Don Tresidder and Mary Curry Tresidder preside at a 1930s Bracebridge Dinner.

*F*or years, it was almost as difficult to obtain tickets for the Bracebridge Dinner as it was to gain admission to Harvard University. Currently, a lottery system for five dinners in three days gives visitors a fighting chance to enjoy fine and memorable music, pageantry, and food. The first celebration on Christmas Day, 1927, was marred, however, by the inebriated state of the Bohemian Club singers who had indulged in a pre-dinner celebration of their own. As the unrehearsed Jester, Ansel Adams, then lean, lanky, and agile, climbed the 40-foot high dining room pillars to, he later admitted ruefully, "the gasps and cheers of diners."

Two years later, the multi-talented Adams collaborated with The Ahwahnee's interior designer Jeanette Dyer Spencer in producing a more appropriate ceremony that enhanced rather than detracted from the environmental and architectural grandeur. It was called the Bracebridge Dinner, as it was an interpretation of author Washington Irving's *Christmas Day at Bracebridge Hall* story.

Mrs. Spencer recorded that her respon-

sibility was to try to "create magic." Her meticulous research and attention to details of settings, costumes, lighting, and stage properties provided glowing enchantment to The Ahwahnee's spacious dining room. Even today, Mrs. Spencer's carefully preserved banners and vibrant Christmas window enhance the room. Her architect husband, E.T. Spencer, was almost equally involved in the production.

Adams' part in the magic was to write the lines for the participants and arrange the music, which ranged from traditional, "Green Groweth the Holly," to triumphal "Wass-aill! Wass-aill! Here's happiness to all..." In addition, he also acted as the majordomo, leading 12 processionals of the choir, and holding the flaming wassail bowl high above his head. Over the years, modifications were made and dramatists from Stanford University replaced local principals. Chorus direction was turned over to Eugene Fulton, and, after his death in 1978, to his daughter Andrea Fulton; nonetheless, the essential drama has remained unchanged.

For more than 40 years, the Spencers

and Ansel Adams put on Bracebridge Dinners with, Adams reflected, "a minimum budget and unlimited imagination." The performances of 1971 were the last for the Spencers, and Ansel retired after the 1972 dinners. In 1979, Virginia and Ansel Adams were invited to sit at the Squire's table, and Adams was pleased that "the quality of the affair had been maintained at a high level by YP&C Co."

Now, as then, after 300-plus guests have been seated in The Ahwahnee's dining room, the Squire leads his lady, a visiting Squire, his wife, and a black-garbed Parson to the raised table at the far end of the Great Hall and bids the assemblage welcome. For the ensuing two-plus hours, beautifully sung carols, and antics of the Bear and Lord of Misrule alternate with elaborate presentations of courses, the Fish, the Peacock Pie, the Boar's Head, the Sirloin of Beef, and finally, the Wassail Bowl and Plum Pudding. Following the Squire's approval of each succulent course, applause rises as waiters and waitresses parade out with trays held high. While guests savor food and drink, entertainment is provided by the jaunty Lord of Misrule, the Bear, or a strolling troubadour. In short, a Bracebridge Dinner is a feast for the eye, ear, palate, and soul.

Left: Majordome Bob Sellby and Ansel Adams as the Lord of Misrule. Above: A featured soloist.

Yosemite's Indian Legacy

Above: 1872 photograph of Yosemite Indians by Edweard Muybridge. Below: Julia Parker and her daughters, Virginia and Lucy, demonstrate basket weaving in the Indian Cultural Museum.

Smoke swirling up from a cooking fire attracts visitors to a winding trail through trees and shrubs in the Indian Village behind Yosemite Valley's Visitor Center. Here, on an ancestral camp site, stand cedar bark *u-ma-chas* (homes), a *chuck-ah* (acorn granary), a *hangi* or roundhouse (place for ceremonial dancing and prayer), a sweathouse, and an acorn-pounding rock. The re-created village, and the nearby Indian Cultural Museum highlighted by beautifully woven and decorated baskets, are the focus of the Indian Cultural Center. The village was begun in the 1920s when Tabuce, Chief Lemee, and Lucy Tom Telles conducted programs there, then expanded in the 1970s and 1980s by local Indians and the Yosemite interpretative staff.

Representing the Miwok culture of the 1870s, 20 years after their first contact with non-Indians, the village is animated on many a summer day or winter weekend, by Native Americans preparing acorns (a food staple of their diet), and fashioning bows and arrows, as well as weaving baskets. Acorn soup boils in a basket partially filled with hot stones. Traditional skills, ceremonial dances, and hand games are not only demonstrated, but, on certain days, open to participation by Yosemite visitors of all ages.

Leader and guiding spirit of the village is Julia Domingues Parker, a Pomo by birth, but Miwok and Paiute by adoption. Her husband, Ralph Parker, a fullblooded Miwok-Paiute who grew up in Yosemite, can trace his ancestry back five generations. His grandmother, Lucy Tom Telles, 1870s-1956, won a first prize at the 1939 World's Fair with a monumental three-foot diameter basket. Lucy introduced Julia to collecting such native materials as willow, redbud, and fern roots, and weaving them into useful yet artistic baskets.

Julia, who says she was "born under a tree" in Northern California, had a traumatic childhood. At age five, she and her four brothers and sisters were orphaned. Fortunately, they were placed in the home of a German woman who taught them to be proud of their Indian ancestory. This later helped them endure five years in a Bureau of Indian Affairs boarding school in Nevada where they were not allowed to speak their native language or follow any of the Pomo customs. Julia developed a fierce pride, and an ambition to achieve status both as a woman and an Indian. Those characteristics, combined with hard

work, diligence, and vocational training in the school shaped her into a mature woman, wife, mother, retail clerk, and manager of an Indian gift shop.

In 1960, the Park Service asked her to work as an interpreter in the Indian Village. At first, visitors would ask her questions she could not answer, and her ignorance of her own culture made her want to hide behind a basket. Insecurity, pride, and curiosity sent her to the Yosemite Research Library to study, and to the local Indian elders to seek knowledge.

Her hardwon competence gave her authority and composure so that she can now field questions, demonstrate and teach food gathering and preparation, basket weaving, and dancing. Furthermore, she has trained other Indians, including her children and currently her nine grandchildren, to know, respect, and continue the old ways and customs.

It takes skill, patience, and love to select and prepare fibers, create patterns, and weave baskets. Even a "rough" basket takes at least 15 to 20 uninterrupted hours; a fine one can take years. Julia rarely sells her finished work, but in 1983 she presented one treasure to Queen Elizabeth II and Prince Philip during their visit to Yosemite. Other beautiful specimens of her art reside in Oslo, Norway, and the Smithsonian Institution.

When the American Indian Council for Mariposa County was founded in 1971 by Native Americans, including Yosemite residents Jay Johnson and Les James, Julia joined eagerly. The Council's purpose is to preserve and exhibit the culture, customs, and crafts of their ancestry, and to train young people. One of the Council's finest achievements, aided by more than 70 individuals and several organizations, was the building of the Ceremonial Roundhouse, which was dedicated in 1975. A visit to the Indian Village and the Indian Cultural Museum is one of the most rewarding and memorable experiences afforded visitors to Yosemite.

Lucy Tom Telles and one of her superbly crafted baskets.

Our Heritage: Planning for Tomorrow

Above: Ponderosa pinecones on forest floor in Yosemite. Right: The lower Yosemite Fall thunders relentlessly to the Valley floor in springtime.

It took a century of sightseers before visitation to Yosemite exceeded one million in a single year. In 1855, 42 intrepid souls walked or rode in on horseback compared with the one million who arrived by automobile in 1954. Thirteen years later the two-million mark was passed, and in 1987, more than three million people visited the wondrous Park.

Nature continues to shape Yosemite now as it has for millions of years. Occasionally, natural forces such as rockslides interrupt the smooth running of activities, reminding us that we are far from all-powerful. Problems such as traffic congestion in the east end of Yosemite Valley on a few days a year is being reduced by use of free shuttle buses, special bike paths, and a network of one-way roads. A campground reservation system has resolved the problem of congestion caused by long waiting lines at the campgrounds.

Serving the Public

Although the complexities involved in managing today's Yosemite would have been incomprehensible to Galen Clark, John Muir, and the Currys, they are the daily responsibilities of the National Park Service and the concessionaires. The concessionaires' basic role is to serve the public while complying with Park Service regulations and making a fair profit. The Park Service exists to preserve the environment and wildlife, yet provide for the enjoyment of same in a manner that will leave them unimpaired for future generations.

One example of use versus preservation is the recent allowance of river rafting on the Merced River in the Valley. The National Park Service permits rafting during seasonal periods when the water is high but safe, and the concessionaire provides the rafts, paddles, life jackets, and transportation at a reasonable charge.

Rafting is exhilarating and adds to visitor appreciation as the magnificent scenery is viewed from a new perspective. Rafting is operated under the scrutiny of the National Park Service's Resource Management and Visitor Safety divisions. Limits have been set on the number of rental rafts, and their color was changed from yellow to gray so they would be less obtrusive. Private rafts add splashes of color. Each week of the short rafting season, Curry Company employees pick up litter along the river banks and at the end of the season undertake a comprehensive clean-up of the river. Ways to reduce trampling of the river bank at the put-in and take-out points are being studied.

We, the People

Soon after the two-million visitor figure had been reached in 1967, a third and powerful agency became involved in the process of finding new solutions for the complex issues confronting the parks. The public—Yosemite's owners and concerned devotees—demanded a voice in decision-making. Their diverse opinions, expressed by letter, telegram, telephone, and in publications and hearings, were eventually incorporated by the Park Service into a new master plan called the General Manage-

Rafting in Yosemite (top); shuttle bus transportation in the Park (middle); and trail maintenance (bottom). Perfect tranquility (top right) at Cathedral Rocks, Yosemite Valley.

ment Plan (GMP), to address present and future needs of the Park. The 1980 plan called for changes in both management and objectives.

Implementation of the GMP began in 1980 with the landscaping of the mall that stretched from Park Service headquarters to the Degnan's building. Asphalt was replaced in many places by native trees and shrubs, log rounds were moved in for seating, and gradually an attractive mall evolved that now serves visitors both physically and aesthetically.

Each year since then, a variety of major changes have been effected. Some are immediately obvious to the visitor: extension of bikeways, new orientation exhibits, bear-proof food lockers and dumpsters, greater emphasis on biking or using shuttle buses, and renovation of trails. Other major improvements, such as the congressional designation of 89 percent of Yosemite as wilderness, removal of overhead power lines and an old hydroelectric plant, construction of new sewage treatment plants, and the development of better traffic control and public transportation, are not as obvious, but equally important. The reintroduction of bighorn sheep, protective studies of great gray owls, and protection of the peregrine falcon aeries are positive moves toward the balance of wildlife in the Park.

Elimination of private vehicles was a

GMP goal, but constructing the necessarily large satellite parking areas presents new threats to now undisturbed lands. "As design and construction progresses," YNP Superintendent John Morehead says, "we are now becoming painfully aware that there is not enough buildable land at El Portal to accommodate all the proposed facilities and the proposed parking lot. Rethinking, and perhaps, replanning, is unavoidable."

Commitment

Compromises on that and other goals seems inevitable due to environmental and budgetary restrictions, but the commitment to the goal of keeping Yosemite accessible yet protected continues. Spearheaded by its responsive president, Edward C. Hardy, the Yosemite Park and Curry Co. has been actively involved in both cooperative and innovative ways.

In 1983, Curry's warehousing and reservation systems, as well as many employees, were relocated outside the Park. Generous corporate donations aid construction of bikeways, assistance to the local community, preservation of Mono Lake and the Merced River, and other environmental concerns. In 1974, the Curry Company instituted an experimental recycling program for glass, tin, newspaper, aluminum, cardboard, and waste oil that soon proved effective. Two years later, another popular anti-litter, pro-conservation campaign had an immediate and

Above: Sentinel Rock. Top Left:
Oaks in Cathedral Meadow, fall.
Bottom Left: Le Conte Fall,
Tuolumne River, Yosemite.

Top: Dramatic rescue of a hiker at Yosemite Falls. Above: A double rainbow illuminates Half Dome from Glacier Point. Top Right: El Capitan peers through the frozen mist in winter. Bottom: A spectacular view is the reward after a long hike in the high country. Opposite: A heavy snowfall transforms the Three Graces, also called Cathedral Rocks, and the Merced River.

on-going success. Nickel deposits paid on all beverage containers purchased in the Park are refunded when the marked containers are turned in at the recycling centers. In an effort to reduce overall traffic, a free shuttle-bus service is provided by the Company within Yosemite Valley, and to and from Badger Pass during the winter. Seasonal passenger service at reasonable rates also operates to and from Tuolumne Meadows, Wawona, and the Mariposa Grove. Other significant improvements made by the Curry Company include the removal of a pitch and putt golf course at The Ahwahnee, two of the six gas stations in the Park, and several deteriorating buildings used for employee housing. The wood yard, used to prepare firewood for sale, was closed and allowed to revert to nature. A backcountry clean-up project freed some 25 sites of unsightly reminders of people's activities. Old plane wrecks, abandoned weather stations, unused corrals, and a demolished metal bridge were among the debris removed from Yosemite's high country.

A Shared Goal

The precarious balance between use and abuse, progress and preservation, beauty and exploitation has to be frequently adjusted by the Park Service and Yosemite Park and Curry Co. The legion of Yosemite advocates continue to voice strong opinions as to the Park's present and future. These people insist on the right to participate in any future changes. Whether government, concessionaire, resident, or visitor, these sometimes passionate "owners" of Yosemite seek alternatives and solutions to the natural and human problems. For a great many, the multiple diversions and singular splendor of places like Yosemite National Park are as necessary to life as the air we breathe. "Earth has no sorrows that Earth cannot heal," was one of John Muir's beliefs; unfortunately, this is no longer true. Yosemite's guardians, whether official or lay, must remain vigilant and involved to insure the survival of this marvelous park for the awe and enjoyment of future generations.

Visiting Yosemite National Park

Above (top to bottom): Camp Curry; The Ahwahnee Hotel; camping at one of the campsites in Yosemite; The Wawona Hotel. Opposite: Half Dome, seen from the North Rim (top). Climbing in Yosemite (bottom left); Yosemite Valley ice rink (middle); a ranger-led nature walk in Yosemite Valley (right).

Location

Yosemite National Park is located in the heart of California's magnificent Sierra Nevada, 200 miles east of San Francisco. It is easily reached by bus or car on Highway 41 from Fresno, 140 from Merced, and 120 from Modesto. A small fee is charged by the National Park Service to enter the Park.

Information

A Visitor Center is operated year-round by the National Park Service in Yosemite Village. A nature center at Happy Isles and a Visitor Center at Tuolumne Meadows in the high country are open during the summer season. Park visitors are advised to stop by a Visitor Center on arrival. Information is available on weather, trail, and road conditions throughout the Park. The Yosemite Association, a non-profit funding group working closely with the Park Service, operates a book store in the Visitor Center. The Association also assists the Park Service in maintaining a permanent general-interest exhibit on the Park in the Center, along with changing temporary exhibits of topical interest.

Both the National Park Service and the Yosemite Park and Curry Co. offer varied interpretive programs to enhance visitor appreciation and enjoyment of the Park. Information on ranger talks, special hikes, movies on Yosemite, and self-guiding trails and exhibits in the Park can be obtained from the current *Yosemite Guide*, handed to visitors entering the Park, and at the Visitor Center. In addition, all Park lodging has front-desk information on activities in Yosemite.

Accommodations

Accommodations range from tents, tent cabins, and motel-style units to rooms at the historic Ahwahnee and Wawona Hotels. For all accommodation, other than campgrounds, early advance reservations from the Yosemite Park and Curry Co., Yosemite National Park, CA 95389, tel: (209) 252-4848, are advised.

All Valley campgrounds are by reservation only. Reservations should be made eight weeks in advance through Ticketron. Some campgrounds outside the Valley are also by reservation only. Others operate on a space-available basis. Fees and facilities vary, and most of the camps are open only seasonally from May/June to September/October. No hook-ups are available.

Food Services

Appetites increase in the mountains, and there are meal options in Yosemite to suit nearly every budget and taste. Hearty fare is offered at Yosemite Lodge's two restaurants, and in Yosemite Village at the Loft Restaurant above Degnan's Deli. Cafeteria-style service is available daily at Curry Camp and Yosemite Lodge. Degnan's Deli is a popular fast-food outlet, serving pizza and sandwiches, among other deli items. Hamburger stands in the Village and Camp Curry also offer fast foods. At the other end of the scale, superb dining with a view is offered in The Ahwahnee Hotel's magnificent dining room, and outside the Valley, at the historic Wawona Hotel. Excellent family-style meals are the summer fare at the six high country camps. White Wolf and Tuolumne Meadows Lodges offer memorable menus during the summer. Restaurants in some locations operate on a seasonal basis; schedules can be found in the free *Yosemite Guide* obtainable in the Park.

Activities

More than 700 miles of trails of varying difficulty are used by walkers, backpackers, and horses, who have the right of way. Saddle and pack animals can be rented seasonally at stables in Yosemite Valley, White Wolf, Tuolumne Meadows, and Wawona. Yosemite has the largest rental stable operating in any national park. During winter, downhill skiing takes place at Badger Pass, 20 miles from Yosemite Valley. Cross-country skiing and snowshoeing are popular on miles of snow-covered roads and trails. Ice skating is available on the rink in Yosemite Valley.

Yosemite is a rock-climber's paradise. Climbers on El Capitan and Half Dome, as well as on other sheer faces, can be seen much of the year. A mountaineering school is operated in the Valley, and at Tuolumne Meadows seasonally. More leisurely pursuits such as golf on the Wawona Hotel's nine-hole golf course, and fishing on the Merced River are always favorite pastimes. Bird watching is a successful activity in Yosemite, as there are several hundred different species of birds to spot. Many people, however, come to Yosemite simply to contemplate the beauty of nature—an ever-changing, seasonal joy.

Tips

To get the most from your stay in Yosemite, try to plan your trip in advance. Preferred accommodations may not be available if you wait until you arrive in the Park to reserve lodging. Be sure to bring clothing suitable for a change in the weather; the Sierra is known for its sudden thunderstorms and temperature changes. Layered clothing is preferable, with at least one sweater and a waterproof jacket. Lightweight hiking boots or running shoes are recommended, as the best way to see the Park is on foot. Almost anything you may need will probably be available in the Park, including medical services, a gas station, and a garage, but it is advisable to come prepared with what you think you might need.